A Manual Of Gesture: Embracing A Complete System Of Notation, Together With The Principles Of Interpretation And Selections For Practice, By Albert M. Bacon. [rev. And Enl.]

Albert M. Bacon

A

MANUAL OF GESTURE;

EMBRACING A COMPLETE

SYSTEM OF NOTATION,

TOGETHER WITH THE

PRINCIPLES OF INTERPRETATION

AND

SELECTIONS FOR PRACTICE.

By ALBERT M. BACON, A. M.
PROFESSOR OF ELOCUTION.

" Association's mystic power combines
Internal passion with external signs."
LLOYD'S ACTOR.

CHICAGO:
S. C. GRIGGS AND COMPANY.
1875.

PREFACE.

Agreeable sounds and harmonious action — one addressing the ear, and the other the eye — combine to perfect the orator.

In the department of vocal culture there is no lack of text-books. Dr. Rush, in his masterly work entitled *The Philosophy of the Human Voice*, has furnished the most ample facilities for the cultivation of the vocal powers; and for those who find his book too elaborate, Prof. William Russell has published his *Orthophony : or, Vocal Culture*, in which the subject is rendered simple and practical. These, and other similar works, furnish the requisite means of acquiring the principles and rules of vocal culture.

With respect to the department of gesture, however, the case is far different. The want of a complete text-book is seriously felt by the student of oratory. To this want the deficiency of public speakers quite generally, in regard to this subject, is mainly attributable.

Among the writers of antiquity, Quintilian, in his *Institutes of Oratory*, has written the most and the best upon this subject.

Rev. Gilbert Austin, an eminent elocutionist of London, issued in A. D. 1806 his *Chironomia*, a quarto volume of six hundred pages, more than two-thirds of which is devoted to the subject of gesture. This is the most valuable as well as the most extensive, treatise ever written upon this branch of oratory.

The present volume is based upon the work of Mr. Austin. The system of notation here adopted is substantially the same as that invented by him, and contained in the *Chironomia*. As regards the interpretation of gesture, which is a prominent feature of this work, the author claims to have more fully developed and thoroughly systematized this branch of the subject than any other author has attempted to do.

This Manual was originally prepared, in manuscript, for the use of my own pupils while engaged in teaching elocution in New England. A limited edition was afterwards published in pamphlet form. The work has now been carefully revised, much enlarged, and illustrated with cuts. In the interpretation of gesture, new definitions and new combinations, with more copious examples, have been added.

I am much indebted to Prof. William Russell, the eminent elocu tionist and accomplished scholar, for his hearty co-operation and valuable suggestions in the preparation of this volume. Both from his published works and from frequent personal interviews, I have received important aid.

A. M. BACON.

Chicago, *Nov.* 30, 1872.

CONTENTS.

———

1*

CHAPTER I.

RHETORICAL DELIVERY.

Rhetorical Delivery includes the management of the voice, the gesture, the attitude, and the expression of the countenance.

The advantage of a natural, graceful, and effective delivery is second in importance only to the sentiments and language of a public speaker. Indeed, so great have been the achievements of the oratorical art, so marked the success of those who have thoroughly cultivated it, as contrasted with others of equal, or even superior talents in other respects, but deficient in this, that many have been led to attach more importance to delivery than to composition. The public speaker who neglects this part of an orator's education certainly suffers great loss. He may be esteemed for his learning, and command the appreciation of those who listen to his wise and judicious sayings, who admire the many excellencies of his production, and he may rest satisfied with this measure of success; but the added power of a winning and persuasive delivery would greatly increase the efficiency of his public efforts.

The words of Cicero, coming down through the centuries, should have weight with us in our compara-

tive neglect of this subject. In his work on celebrated
orators he says: "It is of little consequence that you
prepare what is to be spoken, unless you are able to
deliver your speech with freedom and grace. Nor is
even that sufficient, unless what is spoken be delivered
by the voice, by the countenance, and by the gesture
in such a manner as to give it a higher relish." Refer-
ing to the tones of voice, to gesture, and the expression
of the countenance, he says: "It is hardly possible to
express of how great consequence is the manner in
which the orator avails himself of all these. For even
indifferent speakers, by the dignity of their action,*
have frequently reaped the fruits of eloquence; whilst
those whose language is that of an orator, often on
account of the awkwardness of their action, have been
reckoned indifferent speakers."

Quintilian, also, in his observations upon Hortentius,
says: "If delivery can produce such an effect as to
excite anger, tears, and solicitude in subjects we know
to be fictitious and vain, how much more powerful must
it be when we are persuaded in reality? Nay, I venture to pronounce that even an indifferent oration,
recommended by the force of action, would have more
effect than the best if destitute of this enforcement."
Again he says: "Unquestionably, since mere words
have, in themselves, a powerful efficacy, and since the
voice adds to what is said its own influence, and since
gesture and emotion have also their peculiar signifi-

---

* It should be here observed that, with the ancients, *action* was synonomous
with *delivery*, and embraced voice, gesture, attitude, and facial expression. We use
the term to indicate only that part of delivery which addresses itself to the eye.

cance, something perfect must be produced when all are combined together."

The acknowledged ability of Lord Chesterfield to judge in such matters will give weight to the following quotation from him: "If you would either please in a private company or persuade in a public assembly, air, looks, gestures, graces, enunciation, proper accents, just emphasis, and tuneful cadences, are full as necessary as the matter itself."

The importance of a good delivery may be considered with reference to three departments of oratory: Deliberative, Judicial and Sacred. The other purposes which the art may be made to serve will be found nearly related to one or another of these.

The statesman, who in some measure is held responsible for the welfare of the state, needs to supplement other qualifications with such oratorical resources as shall not only fit him for the ordinary demands of public service, but render him equal to any emergency. Amidst the turmoil of revolution or the conflict of nations, it may be his mission to roll back the tide of war, and, like the son of Hermes,

> " With siren tongue and speaking eyes,
>   Hush the noise and soothe to peace."

The advocate, who, before judges and jurors, stands to vindicate the rights of his fellow-man, and ofttimes to plead for his life, hazards too much if he ignore the oratorical art. To say nothing of opportunities for rising to eminence in his profession, he may, by the industrious cultivation of this art, render to humanity a far more important service.

But more than all, the minister of the Gospel, whose high vocation is to preach to a lost world the glad tidings of salvation, and lead men to believe in Jesus Christ, that they may be saved from wrath and ruin; the messenger of God who stands between the living and the dead to utter words of such tremendous import as to affect the eternal destiny of every one of his hearers; the bearer of this high and holy commission should most certainly strive for the acquisition of every element of pulpit power. In addition to his faith in God, and the requisite knowledge of the Scriptures, and of men, and of whatsoever things are needful to fit him for his work, and to enable him clearly to illustrate Bible truth, he should by all means labor to possess himself of the undoubted advantages of a powerful and persuasive delivery. In presenting his message, he should at least interpose no obstacle in the way of its easy access to the ear, the vestibule of the soul. He should not weary his congregation by indistinctness of enunciation or want of vocal power; compelling them to expend in the effort to catch the words, that attention which should be given to the thought. He must avoid offending the ear with harsh, or in anywise disagreeable tones, and the eye by ungainly postures, or by awkward, or unmeaning, or superfluous gestures. Above all, he should never grieve the Divine Master, make the angels weep, and disgust his fellow-men by any ostentatious display of his oratory in the pulpit.

More attention to the graces of delivery would augment the power of the modern pulpit. Said Cicero, to some of his learned contemporaries, "It is not genius, it is the genius of oratory that you want." This remark, as well as the following lines from John Byrom, respecting the English clergy, will apply to some theologians of the present day:

> "In point of sermons, 'tis confest
> Our English clergy make the best;
> But this appears, we must confess,
> Not from the pulpit, but the press.
> They manage, with disjointed skill,
> The matter well, the manner ill;
> And, what seems paradox at first,
> They make the best, and preach the worst."

Addison also complains of the general neglect of this subject in his time. He says; "Our preachers stand stock still in the pulpit, and will not so much as move a finger to set off the best sermons in the world. We meet with the same speaking statues at our bars, and in all public places of debate. Our words flow from us in a smooth, continued stream, without those strainings of the voice, motions of the body, and majesty of the hand, which are so much celebrated in the orators of Greece and Rome. We talk of life and death in cold blood, and keep our temper in a discourse which turns upon everything that is dear to us." While this description of English orators may, to some extent, find its counterpart in our own country, the tendency, in many cases, is to the *opposite extreme*. Hamlet's instructions to the players, guarding them against extravagance on the one hand, and tameness on the other, are quite as serviceable to the orator as to the actor:

"Speak the speech, I pray you, as I pronounced it to you, trippingly on the tongue; but if you mouth it, as many of our players do, I had as lief the town crier spoke my lines.   Nor do not saw the air too much with your hand, thus; but use all gently: for in the very torrent, tempest, and (as I may say) whirlwind of your passion, you must acquire and beget a temperance that may give it smoothness.   *   *   *   Be not too tame neither, but let your own discretion be your tutor; suit the action to the word, the word to the action, with this special observance, that you o'erstep not the modesty of nature; for anything so overdone is from the purpose of playing, whose end, both at the first, and now, was, and is, to hold, as 't were, the mirror up to Nature; to show Virtue her own feature, Scorn her own image, and the very age and body of the time his form and pressure.   *   *   *   Now, this overdone, or come tardy off, though it make the unskillful laugh, cannot but make the judicious grieve."

Objections are not unfrequently raised against the systematic study of oratory.   Eloquence, we are told, is the gift of Nature, and must be left to her direction. But Nature, unaided by Art, has never yet produced a perfect orator, nor has she approached perfection.   The great orators of both ancient and modern times have diligently studied the rules of the art until they acquired the grace of cultivated nature.   To say that there is no excellence in this department without the study of rules, would be a libel upon nature and a con-tradiction of history; but to say that the highest excellence can only be attained by the most assiduous culture, is to assert a truth which the history of orators and oratory most fully confirms. The incessant labors of Demosthenes, of Æschines, of Hortentius, of Isocrates, and Gracchus, show that these men agreed with Cicero in the belief that to be an orator, something more is needed than *to be born*.

If it belongs to nature to furnish the world with ready-made orators, why does she not do it? Where are they? Nature will perform her part; but, obviously, it is no more her province to produce finished orators than finished scholars or artists. What every one knows to be true in regard to painting, poetry and music, is also true of oratory: we find in these the bestowment of natural gifts, and the necessity of cultivation; with a degree of attainment proportionate to the industry and perseverance of the recipient.

Some have objected to the study of oratory, on the ground that it tends to form an unnatural style of delivery. In some instances this may be the tendency; but the fault lies not in the art, but in the imperfect acquisition of it. The rules of any art, only partially learned and feebly followed, or even strictly followed without facility of execution, will produce the same result. The meager attention paid to this subject in our literary institutions will never develop the oratorical talent of the country. Twenty-four lessons in vocal culture, interspersed with a few hints on gesture, will hardly suffice to complete the work nature has begun. And yet comparatively few receive even this. Six years is thought to be little enough to devote to the classics; while in the department of oratory, great results are expected from a very small amount of labor.   Six years in Greek, and six weeks in elocution! So long as this is held to be the true relative proportion, we shall continue to hear that elocutionary training tends to unnaturalness; but when this branch of education shall be elevated to its true position, and carried along, side by side, with other branches, we shall hear no more of an objection which applies only to a superficial knowledge of the subject. It is not true that those who have perseveringly devoted themselves to oratory have so signally failed; but, on the other hand, the most natural speakers and actors are known to be the most diligent students of rhetorical and dramatic delivery. According to the position assumed by the objector, Demosthenes, having pursued this study farther than any other man, either in ancient or modern times, should stand out in history as the most mechanical, unnatural and ineffective public speaker that the world has ever produced; but since the great Athenian is universally acknowledged to be the most graceful, natural, and effective among the world's greatest orators, we may well conclude this objection to be unfounded.

We sometimes meet with those who, without special elocutionary instruction, exhibit in their delivery a natural force, freedom and grace, far surpassing many others who have devoted themselves to this department. Some have construed this into an argument against the systematic study of oratory. But the argument proves too much. It bears with equal force against other branches whose utility is unquestioned. There are mathematical geniuses who can accomplish more without the rules of the science than many others can with them. The same is true of other branches of learning. But shall they all, on this account, be discarded? If not, why then single out and make an exception with respect to oratory?

There have been men who never pursued a college course, and yet such have been their achievements in life that their names will survive those of the great majority of graduates a thousand generations, and even outlive the names of all the colleges of their time. But who would think of mentioning this as an argument against the utility of colleges? Because nature has bestowed peculiar gifts upon a few, shall we, therefore, say that there is no acquired excellence? As well condemn the science of agriculture because some soils yield more spontaneously than others do with the most careful cultivation. But let it be remembered that those who are by nature endowed with the highest oratorical talents will achieve the most brilliant success in the diligent study of eloquence; as that soil which is naturally most productive, will most richly reward its liberal cultivator.

The success of those who have applied themselves to the study of oratory fully attests the value of the art. Among these, Demosthenes ranks the highest. For the encouragement of those who look upon a high degree of excellence in this department as the peculiar mark of genius, and, therefore, unattainable by them, it may be mentioned that it was only by great perseverance, and after repeated and mortifying failures, that Demosthenes succeeded at all. Plutarch relates of him that, upon one occasion, while complaining to Satyrus of his want of success, notwithstanding his continued efforts, the latter asked him to recite some lines of Euripides or Sophocles. When he had complied, Satyrus repeated them over after him, but with such tones and gestures as to show the value of elocutionary training. "And being persuaded how much of ornament and grace is added to the speech by the delivery, he considered of little or no value the labor of any man who neglected the pronunciation and the gesture suited to the words." Accordingly, he built a subterranean study, in which he daily exercised his voice. Here he would remain for two or three months at a time, and he even shaved one side of his head that he might compel retirement. The success of Demosthenes furnishes the most illustrious example on record of what may be accomplished by close and continued application. Such was the esteem in which he was held by his own countrymen that, " when he was to plead, all ingenious men flocked to Athens from the remotest parts of Greece, as to the most celebrated spectacle of the world." The Romans also regarded him with the highest admiration, as may be inferred from the exclamation of Cicero: "Let us imitate Demosthenes! * * * What else, I beseech you, do we attempt, or what more do we wish? Yet, still, we shall never reach his perfections!" The mere reading of his orations conveys no adequate idea of the effect produced by their delivery. Says Valerius Maximus: "In Demosthenes, is wanting a great part of Demosthenes, since he must be read and cannot be heard."

Cicero, who enjoyed a reputation in Rome, similar to that of Demosthenes in Greece, seems to have exemplified his own definition of eloquence,— *The art of gaining others to our opinions.* His biographer tells us that no other ancient orator could so easily and naturally turn the feelings of an audience in any desired direction. With his consummate oratory, he electrified the Roman senate. By the power of his eloquence, he delayed for a time the downfall of the Republic.

The success of Cicero, like that of Demosthenes, was the result of close application to the study of rules, and persevering practice in the art of delivery. " They were the most assiduous, the most rigorous, the most literal self-cultivators, in the humblest and minutest details, of practical elocution."

Æschines, a celebrated Athenian orator, and rival of Demosthenes, excelled in extemporaneous oratory, of which he was called the inventor. Being at the head of one of the political parties of Attica, he had many fierce contests with Demosthenes, who was the leader of the opposite party. Demosthenes himself acknowledged the agreeable quality and volume of his rival's voice, and the graces of his manner in the tribune. Æschines afterwards founded a school of oratory at Rhodes, which became celebrated throughout the world.

Hòrtentius, a personal friend of Cicero, although not possessed of the highest order of talents in other respects, was, on account of the graces of his delivery, accounted the rival of Cicero. Quintillian says "there was something in him which strangely pleased when he spoke, which those who perused his orations could not find."

William Pitt, so distinguished in the British Parliament for his majestic and overpowering eloquence, acquired his power of extemporizing by a severe course of training at Oxford, where he gained a high reputation, not only for talent, but for skill in elocution. It is said that after entering parliament he remained silent for nearly a year, carefully studying the character of the house. For the following description of Pitt we are indebted to Lord Macaulay:—"His figure, when he first appeared in parliament, was strikingly graceful and commanding, his features high and noble, his eyes full of fire. His voice, even when it sank to a whisper, was heard to the remotest benches; when he strained it to its full extent, the sound rose like the swell of the organ of a great cathedral, shook the house with its peal, and was heard through the lobbies and down staircases, to the Court of Requests and the precincts of Westminster Hall. He cultivated all these eminent advantages with the most assiduous care. His action is described by a very malignant observer as equal to that of Garrick. His play of countenance was wonderful; he frequently disconcerted a hostile orator by a single glance of indignation or scorn. Every tone, from the thrilling cry to the impassioned aside, was perfectly at his command."

The younger Pitt, for a considerable time the leading spirit in the House of Commons, was also distinguished for his oratorical accomplishments. It is said that " he could pour forth a long succession of round and stately periods without premeditation, without ever pausing for a word, without ever repeating a word, in a voice of silver clearness, and with a pronunciation so articulate that not a letter was slurred over." We are told that his father had trained him from infancy in the art of managing his voice, which was naturally clear and deep-toned, and that his whole education had been directed to the point of making him a great parliamentary orator.

The eloquence of Fox was of that higher type which consists of "reason and passion fused together." Mackintosh says:—"He certainly possessed above all moderns that union of reason, simplicity and vehemence which formed the prince of orators. He was the most Demosthenean speaker since Demosthenes." Says Dr. Johnson: "Here is a man who has divided a kingdom with Cæsar, so that it was a doubt which the nation should be ruled by, the sceptre of George III, or the tongue of Mr. Fox." Edmund Burke calls him "the most brilliant and successful debater the world ever saw," an opinion which was admitted even by his enemies.

Lord Erskine, acknowledged to be the greatest of English advocates, is another example of the success attending the study of oratory. His eminence, it is true, was suddenly achieved, but was, nevertheless, the result of previous preparation. We are told that he studied some of the best models of oratory till he almost knew them by heart, and also passed many evenings in a debating association, where, after the example of Pitt and Burke, he trained his talents to that surpassing

strength which afterward gained him the high reputation he enjoyed as an advocate. One source of Erskine's
power over a jury, lay in his extraordinary ability to
read the countenances of his hearers, and adapt himself
to their varying emotions.

A remarkable instance of native genius, combined
with self-culture, is found in the extraordinary history
of Patrick Henry.   With little aid from the schools, he
rose head and shoulders above his contemporaries, and
roused three millions of people to the cry of " *Liberty or
death !*" He was recognized as " the champion of consti-
tutional liberty," and " the mouth-piece of the Revolution."   According to his own account, the first oratorical
aspirations of young Henry were awakened at the age
of fourteen, while listening to the wonderful eloquence
of Rev. Samuel Davies, the great orator of the Presby-
terian church.   We afterwards find him studying
human nature while engaged in his father's store ; ex-
citing debates among the country people who frequented
the place, relating stories and anecdotes, and then de-
ciphering the various emotions expressed in their countenances.   By such methods he doubtless acquired that
knowledge of the passions and their outward signs,
which enabled him in so extraordinary a manner to
express feeling by a simple movement of the features.
" The stern face would relax and grow soft, pensive,
and gentle ; or a withering rage would burn in the fiery
eye ; or eyes, mouth and voice would convey to the
listener emotions of the tenderest pathos."   Hence, he
was enabled to influence, as he did, the minds of jurors,
over whom he is said to have exercised " a species of

magnetic fascination which took their reason captive, and decided the result without reference to the merits of the case." His eloquence has been described as " Shakespeare and Garrick combined."

Henry Clay was, unquestionably, the most consummate orator of his time. The charm of his eloquence was felt even beyond the line of personal contact. Multitudes who never heard the sound of his voice, were drawn by his magnetic influence. Without being elected to the highest official position, Henry Clay, like Daniel Webster, rose majestically above that position. But for the clashing of opinions, but for political prejudices and party preferences, the eloquence of Clay would have won every heart in the nation. Aside from his pure and lofty patriotism, he possessed that rare faculty, which, if made the test of eloquence would so far modify Cicero's definition as to make it *the art of winning others to ourselves.* The great Kentuckian won his hearers first to himself, and then to his opinions. Such was the suavity of his address, that an eminent political antagonist is said to have refused an introduction to him lest he should be " magnetized and mollified, as others had been, by personal contact."

Clay began early in life to cultivate his speaking powers. We give his own language addressed to a graduating class of law students: " I owe my success in life to one single fact, namely, that at an early age I commenced, and continued for some years, the practice of daily reading and speaking the contents of some historical or scientific book. * * * * It is to this early practice of the art of all arts that I am indebted

2

for the primary and leading impulses that stimulated my progress, and have shaped and moulded my entire destiny."

The eloquence of Daniel Webster was the eloquence of matter rather than manner. Some one has said that "his words weighed a pound apiece." His speeches read better than Clay's. In the senate Webster was the thunder, Clay was the lightning. Webster was distinguished for force and earnestness; hence he made frequent use of the clinched hand, "the sledge-hammer gesture." Clay's delivery was remarkable for ease and grace. His favorite gesture was the pointing finger. One of his hearers remarked that his arguments seemed to drop from the end of his finger.

The oratory of Edward Everett combined, in a very high degree, the exquisite finish of the writer with the artistic culture of the speaker. What Cicero says of Hortentius may be said of Mr. Everett, that his delivery had "even more of art than was sufficient for an orator." His action was "faultily faultless."

Those who speak without regard to the rules of art would do well to study such a model as Mr. Everett; while those who are faulty in the opposite direction— whose delivery exhibits more conformity to rules than freedom and grace—had better study John B. Gough, who may be styled Edward Everett's oratorical antipode.

Wendell Phillips ranks among the foremost of American orators. His delivery is simple and natural; conversational rather than declamatory. His musical voice and graceful action give pleasure to the ear and the eye. He always interests his audience, not only because he has something to say, but because of the ease and grace with which he says it. When fully aroused upon great occasions, he carries everything before him. Mr. Phillips' manner before an audience is earnestly recommended to those public speakers who are exhausting themselves by over-exertion. By adopting a moderate style of delivery, many a man might regain his wasted energies, and make the business of speaking what it should be, a healthful exercise both for body and mind.

John B. Gough's oratory is emphatically *sui generis.* Its like is not to be found in either hemisphere. His marvelous influence over an audience is due to his knowledge of human nature, his faith in mankind, his power of imitation and description, added to his warm and generous sympathies—the orator's touch-stone, the key to the popular heart. As regards his style of delivery, Mr. Gough may be said to be above rules. The exacting professional elocutionist may find much to criticize; but to confine such a man as Gough to the rules of the schools, would be unwise; and to make those rules the test of his merit, would be unjust.

The pulpit presents the widest and the most productive field for the exercise of oratorical talent. The themes here discussed are not only inexhaustible, but they are the most elevating that can possibly employ the human mind. The sacred orator, therefore, has an immense advantage over the secular. If the orators of Greece and Rome carried their art to so high a degree of perfection, and produced such wonderful results before the introduction of Christianity, how great should be the success of those who discourse upon the exalted themes of the Christian religion.

Pulpit oratory derives its importance from the consideration that preaching is the divinely appointed means of saving men.

The most eloquent preacher in the early church was Chrysostom, "the golden-mouthed," who was a diligent student of the Greek masters of oratory. One of the most remarkable examples of pulpit eloquence on record is that of George Whitefield, whose preaching attracted vast multitudes, both in England and America. He combined in an eminent degree a natural grace of manner and highly cultivated oratory with that holy zeal which is the highest type of eloquence. "His voice," says Southey, "excelled both in melody and compass, and its fine modulations were accompanied by that grace of action which he possessed in an eminent degree, and which has been said to be the chief requisite of an orator." Says another writer: "His voice was marvelously rich, sweet and sonorous. His eloquence has rarely been surpassed. It was a natural gift improved by diligent study. * * * * His gestures and the play of his features were full of dramatic power." This advantage he doubtless gained from Garrick, from whom it is stated he took lessons.

To his natural gifts and graces Whitefield added the power which lay hidden in his favorite maxim, to preach as Apelles painted, for *eternity*. "Would ministers preach for eternity," he says, "they would act the part of true Christian orators, for then they would endeavor to move the affections and warm the heart, and not constrain their hearers to suspect that they dealt in the false commerce of unfelt truth."

In the education of an orator the elements of delivery should first be taught separately, and then combined in reading and declamation. After being thoroughly drilled in articulation, and properly instructed in the management of the breath, so as to speak without difficulty, and without injury to the vocal organs, the student should attend carefully to the various elements of speech; as quality, force, stress, time, pitch and slide; as well as to attitude, gesture, and the expression of the countenance. He should so thoroughly master all these as to be able to dismiss from the mind every thought of rules while in the act of speaking. Prescribed rules are but the scaffolding which is to be removed when the building is finished. The rules of delivery, like those of grammar and rhetoric, should be so familiar to the orator as to be strictly observed, while the mind is wholly engrossed with the subject-matter. Then may we look for

> " The grace of action, the adapted mien,
>   Faithful as nature to the varied scene ;
>   Th' expressive glance, whose subtle comment draws
>   Entranced attention, and a mute applause ;
>   Gesture that marks with force and feeling fraught ;
>   A sense in silence, and a will in thought :
>   Harmonious speech, whose pure and liquid tone
>   Gives verse a music, scarce confessed its own."

Let no one suppose that real eloquence can be attained by mere conformity to the rules of art. Art produces the body of eloquence, which, however well formed and beautiful in its outward appearance, must, nevertheless, have breathed into it the breath of life. Eloquence, which is the culmination of oratory, has been defined as " logic on fire."   Daniel Webster says of it, " It comes, if it come at all, like the outbreaking of a fountain from the earth, or the bursting forth of volcanic fires, with spontaneous, original, native force."

The study of oratory evidently presupposes a knowledge of such branches as are needful to supply the orator with subject-matter, and also an acquaintance with the structure of language, the principles of logic, and the rules of composition; and yet all these possessed in the highest degree, and combined with the graces of the most finished oratory are, of themselves, insufficient to make true eloquence.   They need to be supplemented with still higher qualities.   To quote again from Webster, there must be " the high purpose, the firm resolve, the dauntless spirit, speaking on the tongue, beaming from the eye, informing every feature, and urging the whole man onward, right onward to his object."

But since these conditions may be met, the student has no occasion to despair.   The advocate is supposed to be sufficiently zealous for his client, the legislator for his country, and the minister of Christ for a lost world, as to inspire all these with genuine eloquence.

CHAPTER II.

GESTURE.

Gesture embraces the various postures and motions of the body; as the head, shoulders and trunk; the arms, hands and fingers; the lower limbs and feet. It is the language of nature; and hence, like the expression of the countenance is a universal language. While the spoken or written language of one nation must be learned by the people of another before they can communicate with each other in words, these visible signs are understood by all alike. A verbal threat has a different word for each nationality; but the uplifted clinched hand and the angry look has the same meaning in all countries. So in the expression of friendly feeling. The assurance of good will spoken in the ear of a foreigner may be utterly misapprehended; while the outstretched hands accompanied with a conciliatory attitude and genial countenance are quite intelligible.

This subject is well illustrated by the ancient pantomimes, who, without the aid of words, recited entire dramas, and delivered the various fables of the gods and heroes of antiquity, making their gestures perfectly intelligible to the whole Roman people, as well as to foreigners. It is related that a barbarian prince visiting

Rome in Nero's time, after witnessing one of these exhibitions, requested the Emperor to allow him to take home with him the principal actor, saying that he had many visitors from neighboring provinces whose language he could not understand, that it was difficult to procure interpreters, and he thought that by the aid of this pantomime he could easily make himself understood by all.

In like manner the deaf mute communicates by visible signs; and the infant knows a smile from a frown long before words have any meaning. It not unfrequently happens in a public assembly that some forcible or significant gesture makes a deeper impression than the language which accompanies it.

In order to persuade men and move them to action, it is obviously better to address the eye and the ear than the ear alone; and if so, then it should be done in the best manner possible. With the hands, to which Quintilian attributes the faculty of universal language, we invite or repel, accept or reject, give or withhold, welcome or deprecate. By them we indicate number and quantity, and express abundance or destitution, exultation or dejection. With a motion of the hand we appeal, challenge, warn, threaten and scorn. In the Egyptian hieroglyphics language is symbolized by a hand placed under a tongue. Cressolius speaks of the hand as " the admirable contrivance of the divine artist —the minister of wisdom and reason;" and adds, " Without the hand no eloquence."

The organic connection of the vocal powers with certain muscles of the body demands the employment of gesture as an accompaniment of animated speech. Oratorical speaking is a compound motion of the lungs, the muscles of the glottis, and of the abdomen; and, when accompanied with gesture, the muscles of the chest also. It is manifest that the action of these muscles should be corellated with appropriate tones and gestures; this corellation takes place in the emphatic utterance of the following command:

"Forward, the Light Brigade!"

the hand being thrown forward simultaneously with the forcible expulsion of the voice.

The necessary connection between muscular and nervous action should also be recognized, and turned to account by the orator. On the one hand, nervous excitement expresses itself by the muscles of the body; on the other hand, the nervous system is aroused by muscular exertion. The lethargic speaker may, therefore, wake himself up by an energetic period of gesture.

The degree of perfection to which the art of gesture was carried by the ancients is shown from the challenge of Cicero by Roscius, the latter contending that he could express the same idea in a greater variety of ways by his gestures than the former could by the use of words.

It is to be regretted that this art, as perfected by the old masters of Greece and Rome, was not preserved, that along with their orations we might study their style of delivery; but they seem to have had no method of recording either tones or gestures, and hence the eloquence with which it is said they "shook distant

2*

thrones, and made the extremities of the earth tremble," must be reckoned among the lost arts.

" The pliant muscles of the various face,
 The mien that gave each sentence strength and grace,
 The tuneful voice, the eye that spoke the mind,
 Are gone, nor leave a single trace behind."

By the aid of a system of notation, such as Mr. Austin has given us in his Chironomia, the entire action of an orator may be faithfully recorded. Gesture is thus reduced to a science; and the student is relieved from the necessity of inventing for himself a system of action which, to say the least, is a needless " waste of ingenuity," at well as of time.

In the general classification of Gesture we have:

I. Designative or Discriminating Gestures, used for indicating or pointing out, and for discriminating between different objects. These may employ the index finger:

Ex.—Thou art the man; (Fig. 81.)

Or the open hand:

Ex.—I refer the matter to these friends at my right. (Fig. 16.)

II. Descriptive Gestures, which serve to describe objects and to represent numbers and space:

Ex.—Darkness covered the entire land.

Here the outward sweep of the prone hands, to the line *horizontal lateral*, describes the act of covering, and also shows the extent of the darkness. (*See fig.* 49.)

III. Significant Gestures; such as placing the hand on the head to indicate distress, or the finger on the lips to enjoin silence; throwing up the hands to express surprise, or reaching them forward in supplication; dropping the head in shame, or holding it up in pride, or nodding in assent or salutation; bending the body forward in reverence, throwing it back in pride, or holding it erect in courage; advancing in entreaty, retiring in fear, starting in terror, and stamping in authority,—these and similar postures and motions fall under the head of Significant Gestures, the most of which are called attitudes.

IV. Assertive Gestures; employed not for designation or description, but for mere assertion, either emphatic or unemphatic; as, "The laws must be obeyed." (*See figs*. 8, 9.)

V. Figurative Gestures, or Gestures of Analogy. The interpretation of these is based upon the analogy between mere physical, and intellectual or moral conditions. The expression of ideas by means of visible signs necessarily involves this principle. For an illustration, apply the same gesture to the following sentences:

1. This is the letter I brought you.
2. This is the subject we are to consider.

Here the same position and movement of the hand presents, first, a visible object, and then a mental proposition.

Compare the following examples:

1. Arrest that criminal.
2. Arrest that fugitive thought.

In this case we employ the gesture *right hand horizontal front prone*, to describe both the physical act and the corresponding mental conception. (*See fig.* 36.)

Notice also the following:

1. We deposit this body in the earth.
2. All personal feeling he deposited upon the altar of his country.

Both the physical and the moral idea of deposition are here expressed with *both hands descending front supine.* (*Fig.* 22.)

This analogy may be quite remote.

Ex.—1. The youth wandered far from the parental roof.
2. Blind unbelief is sure to err.

To err is to wander from the truth; hence we assign to the second, as well as to the first, the gesture of wandering—*right hand horizontal lateral supine.* (*Fig.* 16.)

Whether an idea is expressed literally or figuratively, the gesture is the same.

The student will observe the coincidence between the class of gestures last mentioned and some of the preceding. A gesture of analogy, for instance, may also be a descriptive gesture. Take the example, " Darkness covered the entire land; " substitute spiritual for literal darkness, and the gesture is purely figurative, but no less descriptive than before.

By another principle of division, gestures may be classified according to the style of delivery. Mr. Austin gives three different styles: Epic, Rhetorical and Colloquial; and describes the various qualities which belong to them. The qualities of gesture, as enumerated by him, are Magnificence, Boldness, Energy, Variety, Simplicity, Grace, Propriety, and Precision. The following descriptions are, for the most part, taken from the Chironomia:

Magnificence of Gesture consists in the ample space

through which the arm and hand are made to move. The motions of the head are free, and the inflections of the body manly and dignified, and the feet traverse a considerable space with firmness and force. The opposite faults are short and constrained gestures, with stiffness of the body, and doubtful or timid movements.

Boldness consists in that elevated courage and self-confidence which ventures to hazard any action productive of a grand or striking effect. In this sort of gesture, unexpected positions, elevations and transitions, surprise at once by their novelty and grace, and thus illustrate or enforce ideas with irresistible effect. The opposite fault is tameness, which hazards nothing, and is timid and doubtful of its powers.

Energy consists in the firmness and decision of the whole action, and in the support which the voice receives from the precision of the stroke of the gesture. The opposite faults are feebleness and indecision.

Variety consists in the ability of readily adapting suitable gestures to each sentiment, so as to avoid recurring too frequently to favorite gestures. The opposite faults are sameness and barrenness of gesture, analogous to monotony of voice.

Simplicity consists in using such gestures as appear the natural result of the situation and sentiments; neither going beyond the just extent of the feelings, nor falling short of it. The opposite fault is affectation.

Grace of Gesture is the result of all other perfections, and consists chiefly in the facility, freedom, variety and simplicity of the action. It is attained by persevering practice after the best models and according to the truest taste. The opposite faults are awkwardness and rusticity.

Propriety, called also Truth of Gesture, or Natural Gesture, consists in the judicious use of those movements which are best suited to the sentiment. The opposite imperfections are false, contradictory or unsuitable gestures.

Precision of Gesture arises from the just preparation, the due force, and the correct timing of the action. The preparation is neither too much abridged nor too pompously displayed. The stroke is made with that degree of force which suits the character of the sentiment and speaker, and occurs on the precise syllable to be enforced. Precision gives the same effect to action that neatness of articulation gives to speech. The opposite faults are the indecision and uncertainty arising from vague and sawing gestures, which obscure the sentiment and distract the spectator.

Epic Gesture requires all these qualities in perfection. The compositions requiring epic gesture are tragedy, epic poetry, lyric odes, and sublime description.

Rhetorical Gesture requires principally energy, variety, simplicity and precision. Grace is desirable; boldness and magnificence may sometimes have place.

Colloquial Gesture principally requires simplicity and grace. Precision will naturally follow. Energy and variety may be sometimes demanded; magnificence and boldness are inadmissible. In Colloquial Gesture the elbow instead of the shoulder becomes the center of motion; hence the movements are shorter and less flowing, neither is the action so frequent as in the rhetorical style.

POSITION.—In the study of rhetorical action, Position is the first thing to be attended to. Says Mr. Austin: "Graceful position precedes graceful action." Facility of movement is essential to both; hence the public speaker should stand erect and firm.; not rigid, but easy and natural, with the weight of the body resting mainly upon one foot, so that the other may be readily used in changing the position, as occasion may require. The supporting limb should be straight, and the knee of the other slightly bent.

The positions suited to the ordinary purposes of public speaking are few and simple. They may be designated as follows:

First Position.—Right foot advanced, the left supporting the weight of the body.

Second Position.—Right foot advanced, supporting the body.

Third Position.—Left foot advanced, the right supporting.

Fourth Position.—Left foot advanced, supporting.

The feet should be placed with the toes turned outward, making an angle of about seventy degrees in the retired positions, and ninety in the advanced. The space between the feet should be three or four inches, or about the breadth of the foot. This, however, applies to the positions adapted to reading or to unimpassioned speaking. In impassioned delivery these positions may be so modified as virtually to increase their number. The spaces will be wider, and the angles will vary to suit the purpose of the speaker.

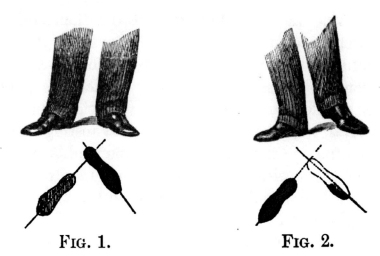

FIG. 1.   FIG. 2.

Figure 1 represents the first position.   The principal weight of the body rests upon the foot that is deeply shaded in the plan.   The other foot, lightly shaded, rests lightly upon the floor.   (*See also fig.* 8.)

The change from the first to the second position is made by stepping forward with the right foot, about half its length, and throwing the principal weight upon it; only that part of the left which is shaded in the plan, as shown in fig. 2, resting upon the floor. (*See also fig.* 9.)   The third and fourth positions are simply the reverse of these.

Earnest appeal, bold assertion, and impassioned speech carry the body forward to one of the advanced positions.

Calm, unimpassioned discourse, also firmness, and resistance, take one of the retired positions.

From each of the positions given above four steps may be made with the foot not supporting the body. The central feet in fig. 3 stand in the first position, the right foot, being free to move, may advance, retire,

traverse to the right and to the left; the various steps
finishing as numbered and shaded in the diagram. The
lines traced by the free foot are each marked with a star.

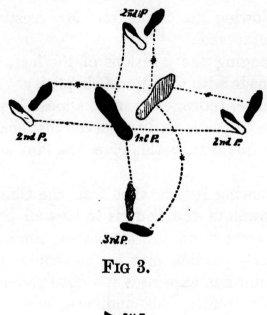

FIG 3.

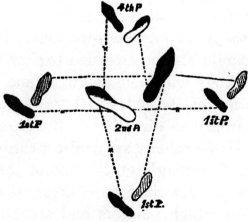

FIG. 4.

Fig. 4 shows the corresponding steps from the second
position. It will be observed that here, in crossing, the

free foot passes behind the other, whereas in crossing from the first position it passes before the other. Neither of these steps should be made except in rare cases.

The following directions from Mr. Austin should be carefully observed:

" In changing the positions of the feet, the motions are to be made with the utmost simplicity. The speaker must advance, retire, or change, almost imperceptibly; and it is to be particularly observed that changes should not be too frequent, as this gives the idea of anxiety, or instability."

The following is also taken from the Chironomia:

" The trunk of the body is to be well balanced and sustained erect upon the supporting limb. Whatever the speaker's position may be, he should present him-self, as Quintilian expresses it—*æquo pectore*—with the breast fully fronting his audience, and never in the fencing attitude of one side exposed. What Cicero calls the *virilis flexus laterum*—the manly inclination of the sides—should also be attended to; for, without this position, the body will seem awkward and ill balanced. The inclination of the sides withdraws the upper part of the body from the direction of the sustaining limb, and inclines it the other way, whilst it throws the lower part of the body strongly on the line of the supporting foot. In this position the figure forms that gentle curve or waving line which painters and statuaries consider as appropriate to grace.

" The gesture of the arms and hands must receive a a slight accompanying movement of the trunk, and not proceed from it as from a rigid log. Whilst care is taken to avoid affected and ridiculous contortions, there must be a manly and free exertion of the muscles of the whole body, the general consent of which, is indispensable to graceful action."

The remarks of Professor Russell will also be serviceable to the student:

" The true time of movement is in exact coincidence with emphasis, and falls appropriately on the accented syllable of the emphatic word. The voice and the bodily frame are thus kept in simultaneous action with the mind. Movement so performed never obtrudes itself on the attention, but becomes a natural part of the whole delivery. The changes of position should always be made (except only the retiring movement, at the close of a paragraph, or of a division of the subject) *during the act of speaking*, and not at the pauses."

The position of the head should be natural and easy; neither so far back as to give the idea of haughtiness, thus showing a want of respect for the audience, nor so far forward as to imply submissiveness and a want of self-respect. The head should move easily, but not rapidly, from side to side.

In the mechanical execution of gesture we employ straight lines and curves; as in geometry, to which the laws of gesture are referable. Straight lines, which indicate directness of thought, are employed to express bold, energetic and abrupt ideas. The curved lines are used in more calm and quiet states of mind, to express gentle and genial thoughts and emotions, and are also adapted to the boldest flights of oratory.

Gestures are quick or slow, and range through large or small space, according to the character of the discourse, and the feelings and circumstances of the speaker. In the unimpassioned, or mere narrative or didactic parts of a discourse, gestures should be few in number, limited in space, and moderate in time; but as the subject gathers interest and the speaker warms, they should be more profuse, varied and energetic. The action should be accommodated also to the size of the room and the number of the audience. The following general directions will be a sufficient guide:

Forcible utterances and vehement emotions are expressed with quick time; calm, quiet, and subdued thoughts and feelings, with slow time.

Solemn and deliberate assertions require large space and slow movement; lively expressions limited space and quick movement.

" The gesture of the public speaker must vary with his circumstances. If the object be merely to instruct his audience, he will limit himself to a very small degree of gesture. He will avoid all parade of preparation, and all the graces of transition, and give only that degree of variety that is necessary to relieve his gestures from sameness. This is far removed from the theatrical, and nearly approaches the colloquial style. When the speaker aims to persuade, and upon extraordinary occasions, he will naturally use more graceful, more flowing, and more varied gestures."—*Austin*.

It is not designed that this study shall necessarily increase the number of gestures which the student has been accustomed to use. What most speakers need is, not a greater number, but a greater variety. The constant recurrence of two or three different motions shows a poverty of resource that may find its remedy in a better acquaintance with the laws of expression. On the other hand many need to study this subject that they may abridge their action, like the awkward youth whose father sent him to the dancing master, that he might learn to stand still.

CHAPTER III.

NOTATION OF GESTURE.

The lines of gesture take three general directions—descending, horizontal, and ascending. Each of these has four subdivisions—front, oblique, lateral, and oblique backwards. The descending gestures carry the hand forty-five degrees below the horizontal line; the ascending, forty-five above. The points designated by the four subdivisions are also forty-five degrees apart. This entire system is represented in *fig.* 5. The vertical lines nearest the speaker (1, 1) are lines in *front;* the next lines—forty-five degrees to the right and left of these (2, 2) are the *oblique;* forty-five degrees farther are the *lateral* (3, 3); and back of these the same distance, the dotted lines (4, 4) are

FIG. 5.

the *oblique backwards*. In the transverse direction the circular lines (5, 6, 7) are called respectively *descending*, *horizontal* and *ascending*. The points where these lines intersect each other, furnish the names of the gestures so far as relates to the direction of the arm ; and these several directions are indicated by the initial letters : d. f., descending front; d. o., descending oblique ; d. l., descending lateral; d. o. b., descending oblique back-wards. The same order is followed on the next line above : h. f., horizontal front, etc. ; and above this we have a. f., ascending front, etc. This gives us twelve gestures with the right hand supine. When the gesture takes the prone or the vertical position of the hand, the letter *p.* or *v.* is added to the notation ; and where both hands are to be employed, this is indicated by prefix-*b. h.*, thus : b. h. d. f. p. is to be read, *both hands descending front prone*. The other combinations will be readily formed from the table of abbreviations.

By thus changing the position of the hands, and executing the gestures with one hand and with both, we have a system embracing fifty-six different gestures (exclusive of thirty-two with the left hand, which are admissible in rare cases). These, executed in various ways—in straight lines and curves, through large and small space, with quick and slow movement, and accompanied with an endless variety of changes in attitude and facial expression, together with the movements denominated special gestures, furnish a vocabulary of gesture commensurate with the realm of thought and feeling.

The descending gestures belong to the sphere of the

Will, and, therefore, predominate in strong resolve and determination, in bold and emphatic assertion, and vehement argumentation.

The horizontal lines belong more especially to the realm of Intellect, and are employed in general thought, and in historical and geographical allusions.

The ascending gestures belong to the Imagination. These are employed in sublimity and general elevation —physical, intellectual and moral.

The gestures in front are generally direct and personal, and also more emphatic than others.

The oblique gestures are more general in their application, and less emphatic than those in front.

The lateral gestures, except in special cases, as in aversion, repulsion, and, it may be, in special designation, are still less emphatic.

The gestures oblique backwards indicate remoteness, and are occasionally used to extend an idea farther than can be well expressed in the lateral line.

The analysis of gesture shows three minor movements: Preparatory, Executionary and Return. These taken together constitute a Period of gesture; or a period may embrace a combination of gestures, beginning with the preparation, extending through a series, and finishing with the return movement.

PREPARATION.—The hand, in preparation for the gesture, is brought up on the oblique line, that is, midway between the front and the lateral. In general, it should not be raised above the head. In lifting the hand, special care should be taken (except in colloquial gestures) to make the shoulder, and not the elbow, the center of motion. In other words, lift the whole arm, and not merely the fore-arm. Let the hand pass through all the space designated by the curved line in fig. 6. In practicing this movement, it is well at first to pause at the horizontal line (2), and then make the angle by bringing the hand to the head (3). The careful observance of this direction will aid very much in securing freedom of action. Indeed, the grace and effectiveness of oratorical action depend largely upon the proper

FIG. 6.

execution of the preparatory movement. It must be well timed, and in harmony with the rhetoric as well as with the sentiment. Except in comic and tragic recitation, there should be no sudden jerking of the arm ; nor, as a rule, should the hand be thrust out without some preparatory action. In demonstration, calm reasoning and simple narrative, where little gesture is needed, and that of a moderate style, the hand should seldom be raised to the head, but may be arrested at any point above the descending line of gesture, according to the sentiment and circumstances. Animated delivery, and especially emphatic utterance, require a corresponding fulness and force of preparation.

EXAMPLES.—I. I cordially *accede* to your request.
r. h. d. f.

Here the hand in preparation is raised scarcely above the terminal point of the gesture.

2. This position I will maintain to the *last*.
r. h. d. f.

This lifts the hand to the head, in order to gain space through which to bring it down with greater emphasis. Compare the uplifted hand in fig. 6 with figs. 8 and 9.

The preparation is also deliberate or rapid, according to the sentiment or the degree of emphasis required.

Ex.—1. Treasurest up unto thyself wrath against the *day* of wrath?
r. h. h. f.

In this case the deliberate lifting of the hand to the head should correspond with the deliberate utterance of the words preceding *day*, upon which the gesture occurs. Prolonged preparation excites attention and enforces gesture.

2. *Freedom* calls you! Quick, be *ready*.
b. h. h. o.

In this example, the hands are suddenly thrown upward on the *first* word; the preparation is then arrested until the *last* word is reached, when they are brought down forcibly upon that word. The uplifting of the hands in this case, as in many others, is both a preparatory and an expressive act. The preparation is sometimes even more expressive than the gesture which follows.

It should be carefully observed that that part of a sentence which precedes the emphatic word usually takes the preparation.

When the gesture occurs upon the *first* word in the sentence, there should be a pause in the voice previous to uttering that word, to allow time for the preparatory action.

Ex.—1. *Fade* flowers! *fade*; nature will *have* it so.
d. o. p.　　rep.　　　　d. a.

2. *Rash, fruitless* war, from *wanton glory* wag'd,
  r. h. d. f. r. h. d. l.   r. h. h. l.
     Is only splendid *murder*.
              b. h. d. f.

3. *What!* threat you me with telling of the *king?*
  h. f.   h. o.

The preparation frequently occurs upon a single syllable, the gesture proper taking the succeeding syllable.

    Ex.—*Away* with *private* wrongs.
      d. l.   imp.

Arrested Preparation.—After the hand is raised in preparation for the gesture, the effect may sometimes be heightened by arresting or suspending the action during a rhetorical pause in speech, or while uttering some significant word, phrase or sentence. The subject of a sentence often requires an arrested preparation, the action being consummated in the predicate. In the following passage:

    " As the heaven is high above the earth, so great is His *mercy*
        toward them that fear Him,"   d. o.

the hand is slowly raised upon the first clause; the preparation is then arrested until the emphatic word is reached, when the hand is brought down to the *descending oblique*. The effect of suspending the action in this manner is analogous to the rhetorical pause in speech.

THE EXECUTIONARY MOVEMENT, or gesture proper, is made upon the emphatic word, phrase or sentence, the *ictus*, or *emphatic stroke*, at the terminus, occurring upon the accented syllable. As the hand approaches its destined point, by an additional movement of the wrist joint it springs with increased velocity to the termination, and thus marks with precision the accented syllable. With respect to the space and time of the action, the same rules which govern the preparation, apply with equal force to the executionary movement. Action not suited to the word is better omitted. A single example will serve to illustrate the importance of correctly timing the gesture:

"Spread wide around the heaven-breathing calm."

Apply to these words the gesture *both hands horizontal lateral prone* (*Fig.* 49), pronouncing very slowly, and then increase the rate of utterance until there is no time for that deliberate movement of the hands which the sentiment requires. It will be seen that with too slow an utterance the gesture is finished too soon for the words; and with rapid speaking the gesture must either be more animated than the descriptive idea will allow, or fall so far behind the words as to appear affected and puerile. "The most flowing and beautiful motions," says Mr. Austin, "the grandest preparations, and the finest transitions of gesture, ill applied and out of time, lose their natural character of grace, and become indecorous, ridiculous, or offensive."

In the RETURN MOVEMENT, after a gesture or a series of gestures is completed, the muscles should relax so as to allow the hand to fall naturally and easily. Like the preparation, this may sometimes serve as an expressive act. Entire cessation or nonentity may occasionally be expressed more effectively by dropping the hand upon certain words, than by any other movement.

Ex.—1. He loosed the steed; his slack hand *fell.*
                                              drop.

2.   Like the lily,
                              d. o.
     That once was mistress of the field, that flourished,
                  h. o.   imp.
     I'll hang my head and *perish*.
                        drop.

3. The time for tender thoughts and soft-endearments
     Is *fled away* and *gone*.   h. l.
        d. l.   drop.

To secure ease and grace of action, all the joints of
the arm and hand—the shoulder, the elbow, the wrist,
and the finger—must move with perfect freedom.
Without the free use of the wrist-joint, particularly,
there can be no grace. The effective execution of the
emphatic stroke at the terminus of the gesture, depends
largely upon the flexibility of the wrist-joint. While
the student of Elocution should study strength and
manliness before grace, he should, at the same time,
carefully avoid *ungraceful* action.

REPEATING THE GESTURE. — When the idea is
repeated, either in the same or in other words, or when
successive reference is made to the same person, place,
or thing, the gesture may be repeated.

Ex.—Which show the works of the law written in their *hearts;* their
     conscience also bearing witness.   r. h. h. o.
        repeat.

This is often done merely for emphasis. The repeated
gesture should then be larger and more forcible than
the first; the preparation carrying the hand higher,
and still higher, as the increasing emphasis demands.

Ex.—1. *On* them, Huzzars! in *thunder* on them wheel!
        b. h. h. f.   repeat.

2. *Charge!* Chester, *Charge! On*, Stanly, *on!*
     r. h. h. f.   rep.   r. h. h. f.   rep.

3. *Nearer, clearer, deadlier* than before.
     b. h d. f.   rep.   rep.

This persistency of gesture, judiciously used, is very effective; but must not be carried into *mannerism*. "Do not saw the air thus."

IMPULSE.—When less emphasis is required, instead of repeating the gesture, there may be a slight *impulse —a repetition of the wrist movement*. The pupil, however, must be cautioned against excess in this direction. The habit of constantly repeating the *ictus* of the gesture is a fault of oratory.

SUSTENTATION OF GESTURE.—After the stroke of the gesture upon the emphatic word, the hand should remain in position until the full effect is produced. To drop it too soon, weakens the gesture.

Ex.—1. I appeal to *you*, sir, for the decision.
r. h. h. f.   sus.

Here the gesture should be sustained until the whole sentence is completed. Keep the hand in the position horizontal front, as if waiting for the decision.

2. How *vain* all outward efforts to supply
r. h. h. l.
The soul with joy!
sus. to the close.

3.   *Tradition's* pages
r. h. h. o. b.
Tell not the planting of the parent tree.
sus.

In the last examples the gesture is sustained beyond the usual limit; when the sentiment admits of it, the effect is heightened thereby. Like the arrested preparation, this may be called a rhetorical pause in gesture.

The following abbreviations embrace the system of notation to be used in recording gesture according to the plan of this Manual. In notating gestures the *s.* may be omitted from the supine hand, and *r. h.* from gestures to be made with the right hand singly, or these may be expressed, at the option of the student. When the position of the hand is not notated, it is to be understood *supine;* and when it is not indicated whether one or both hands are to be used, the *right hand* is understood.

d. f., descending front.
d. o.,   "   oblique.
d. l.,   "   lateral.
d. o. b.,   "   oblique backwards.
h. f., horizontal front.
h. o.,   "   oblique.
h. l.,   "   lateral.
h. o. b.,   "   oblique backwards.
a. f., ascending front.
a. o.,   "   oblique.
a. l.,   "   lateral.
a. o. b.,   "   oblique backwards.
r. h., right hand.
l. h., left hand.
b. h., both hands.
s., supine.
p., prone.
v., vertical.
i. or ind., index finger.
upl., uplifted.
par., parallel.
cli., clinched.
cla., clasped.
ap., applied.
fol., folded.
cro., crossed.
prep., preparation.
rep., repeat.
imp., impulse.
sus., sustain.
tr., tremor.

The initial letters placed under a given word indicate the gesture for that word ; as,

Humility and *modesty* are *cardinal* virtues.
prep.   r. h. h. o. s.   imp.   sus.

This notation indicates that the hand is to be lifted, in preparation for the gesture, upon *humility ;* that the gesture right hand horizontal oblique supine occurs upon *modesty ;* that an impulse of the hand, or partial repetition of the gesture, is made upon *cardinal ;* and that the action is to be sustained to the close of the sentence. This, however, may be abridged. The prepparation and the sustentation seldom need to be notated, and the letters h. o. would suffice, in this case, for the gesture, the right hand supine being understood.

The gestures which a given example is specially intended to illustrate occur upon the CAPITALIZED words. Other gestures in the same example are indicated by the letters placed under the *italicized* words. As a rule, only the former need be noticed at first. After the student shall have gone carefully through the book, executing the gestures occurring upon the capitalized words, and studying their interpretations, he will find great advantage from a review, in which these gestures shall again be executed with their combinations, as indicated by the words in italics.

It will be observed that when no other gesture occurs in the example except the one illustrating the principle under consideration, the notation is omitted, the capital letters being a sufficient guide. When a single gesture is assigned to a phrase or clause, it is intended that the executionary movement shall be made to extend over all the words embraced.

Although different examples are generally given for the different gestures throughout these pages, it will not unfrequently occur that a given passage would be as appropriately expressed with some other gesture than the one assigned to it. This must be determined by the state of the speaker's mind, or by the circumstances in which the language is spoken. Passages ordinarily requiring only a moderate degree of emphasis might, in other circumstances, employ more emphatic gestures. Language in itself unemotional, may, under certain conditions, become highly impassioned, and require corresponding action. The index finger, or even the clinched hand, may then be employed, when at other times the open hand would suffice; both hands may be used instead of one; the straight line may take the place of the curve, and *vice versa*. Indeed, no two persons, however well acquainted with the subject, would be likely to employ precisely the same gestures throughout a given recitation, although they might equally conform to the laws of expression. Differences might arise, not only from different conceptions of the author's meaning in some passage rendered, but from a dissimilarity of temperament, taste, mood, or surroundings.

To suppose that, in every instance, a given sentence or paragraph must necessarily be expressed with a certain style of gesture, and that any deviation from this would be false or inappropriate, would not only be radically erroneous, but would greatly embarrass, if not wholly discourage, the student of oratory. While the general principles laid down in this treatise should govern in the choice of gesture, there is still a wide

3*

margin for the exercise of individual taste and judgment in the matter of suiting the action to the word.

The gestures here described, with their various applications and accompanying examples will, it is believed, if carefully studied, suggest the appropriate style of action in every case that may arise. The subject, however, is of necessity inexhaustible. The student will therefore find ample scope for the exercise of his ingenuity in discovering new combinations, and in bringing out the finer shades of expression.

CHAPTER IV.

RIGHT HAND SUPINE.

FIG. 7.

In these gestures the hand is not entirely supine, but sloping from the thumb about thirty degrees; the fore **finger should** be straight, the others slightly relaxed; the two middle fingers close together and the other fingers somewhat separated from them. The hand should be well opened; when partly closed the gesture is weakened. The palm of the hand, when presented to the audience, possesses great power of expresion.

Right Hand Descending Front Supine.
(FIGS. 8, 9, 10.)

I. This gesture is employed in Emphatic, Particular Assertion, embracing that which is urgent, necessary, inevitable, or impossible.

Regarded as mere assertion, the affirmative and the negative forms are governed by the same law.

FIG. 8. FIG. 9. FIG. 10.

EXAMPLES.—1. This doctrine is founded upon, and consistent with the TRUTH.

2. It MUST be so, Plato; thou reasonest WELL.

3. This preposition must not be entertained for a single MOMENT.

4. The war is INEVITABLE.

5. This can NEVER be.

6. Under existing circumstances war is IMPOSSIBLE.

II. Emphatic Resolve or Determination.

Ex.—1. This sentiment I will maintain with the last breath of LIFE.

2. To such usurpation I will NEVER submit.

III. Imperative or Forcible Demand.

Ex.—1. I demand an immediate SURRENDER.

2. I demand complete REPARATION for the injury.

IV. Emphatic Question, whether Grammatical or Rhetorical.

Ex.—1. Do you POSITIVELY affirm this?

    2. Hath not God made FOOLISH the wisdom of this world?

    3. Why should Rome fall a MOMENT ere her time?

In the foregoing examples the hand is raised to the head and brought down forcibly upon the emphatic word. *See figs.* 8 and 9. In the following, under concession, submission, etc., the hand is but slightly raised in preparation, and the gesture is executed with slow movement. *See fig.* 10. Thus it is shown that in the same notation, a very different, or even opposite effect may be produced by a different mode of execution.

V. Concession ; as,

    I GRANT this principle.

VI. Submission ; as,

    I SUBMIT to your terms.

VII. Humility ;

Ex.—1. I humbly CONFESS my fault.

    2. " Sir," said I, " or Madam, truly your FORGIVENESS I implore."

                              (Mock Humility.)

    3. I kiss the very ground under your FEET.

Before taking up the next gesture in the system— descending oblique—it is well to observe that, in general, the relation of the oblique to the front line of gesture, descending, horizontal and ascending, may be stated thus :

FRONT.	OBLIQUE.
Particular,	General,
Specific,	Generic,
Unity,	Plurality,
Personal,	Impersonal,
Very Emphatic.	Emphatic.

Right Hand Descending Oblique Supine.
(FIG. 11.)

FIG. 11.

I. Emphatic General Assertion, whether affirmative or negative.

EXAMPLES.

1. These are the FUNDAMENTAL principles of knowledge.

2. These things are CERTAINLY true.

3. Of all mistakes none are so FATAL as those we incur through PREJUDICE.
imp.

4. These statements are entirely without FOUNDATION.

5. The assertions of my opponent are false in every PARTICULAR.

II. This gesture, usually in combination with some other, serves to mark with emphasis words opposed to, or compared with each other.

EXAMPLES.—1. What cannot be *prevented*, must be ENDURED.
               h. o.   d. o.

2. What is *done*, cannot be UNDONE.
      h. o.   d. o.

3. There is a material difference between *giving*, and FOR-GIVING.
               h. o.   d. o.

4. He who is *intelligent*, will be INTELLIGIBLE.
      h. o.   d. o.

5. Prosperity *gains* friends, adversity TRIES them.
     h. o.   d. o.

6. We are *weak*, and ye are STRONG.
   h. o.   d. o.

Similar ideas, but more specific, or personal, or delivered with greater emphasis, prefer the line in front; as,

Must we in your person *crown* the author of the public calamities,
              h. f.
or must we DESTROY him?
     d. f.

III. In common with other descending lines, this gesture is used in Consummation and Finality; also to enforce the Predominant Idea. These two applications generally coincide; that is, the predominant idea is emphasized, and the action completed by the same downward stroke.

While the action may be consummated in any line of gesture suited to the sentiment, as shown in many examples in this book, the preference is most frequently given to the descending gestures. The closing idea, by the law of rhetoric the predominant one, is thus marked with force, and the effect rendered more complete; as,

Who builds on less than an *immortal* base,
a. o.
Fond as he *seems*, condemns his joys to DEATH.
h. l.   d. o.

In other circumstances, as when the concluding idea is more emphatic, or when it involves a particular instead of a general assertion, the descending *front* may be the gesture of consummation and finality. The following quotation, closing with an emphatic particular assertion, falls under this head:

I tell you though *you*, though all the *world*, though an angel from
h. f.   h. l.
heaven, should declare the truth of it, I cannot BELIEVE it.
a. o.   d. f.

The *descending lateral* not unfrequently serves to consummate the action, but in cases that are coincident with other uses of that gesture, as explained elsewhere.

In the following examples the descending gesture is employed simply to enforce the predominent idea. The simultaneous consummation of the action is merely incidental:

1. Honor and *virtue*, **nay** even INTEREST demands a different course.
   h. o.   d. o.

2. The *people* demand peace ; yea, the army ITSELF demands it.
   h. o.   d. o.

3. Let any man resolve to do right *now*, leaving *then* to do as it can,
   h. f.   h. o.

   and if he were to live to the age of METHUSELAH, he would
                                           d. o.

   never do wrong.

The following notation serves the same purpose as the above. In this case, however, the direct personal address chooses the line in front :

King *Agrippa*, believest thou the *prophets?*   I KNOW that thou
   h. f.   rep.   d. f.
believest.

IV. General Concession.

Ex.—I CONCEDE these points.

This requires small preparation and slow movement.

V. Submission, Humility, etc.

Ex.—The Turk was dreaming of the hour
   When *Greece*, her knee in SUPPLIANCE bent,
        h. o.   d. o.
   Should TREMBLE at his power.
        imp.

Right Hand Descending Lateral Supine.
(FIG. 12.)

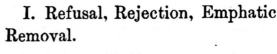

I. Refusal, Rejection, Emphatic Removal.

Ex.—1. I REFUSE the offer.

2. AWAY with an idea so absurd !

Except in rejection, removal, etc., this gesture is generally less emphatic than the descending oblique, but is more emphatic than the horizontal lateral.

II. Negation or Denial.

Ex.—1. The moistened eye, the trembling lip,
   Are not the signs of doubt or FEAR.

FIG. 12.

2. He DISCLAIMS the authority of the king.

3.   To thine own *self* be true,
                h. f.
  And it must follow as the night the *day*,
                       h. o.
  Thou canst not then be false to ANY MAN.
                           d. l.

III. Concession, Relinquishment, Withdrawal, Declension, and kindred ideas.

Ex.—1. I concede ALL THAT MY OPPONENT CLAIMS.

The *wave of concession* makes a full sweep of the hand and arm.

2. Cæsar was an HONORABLE man.

A concession of Mark Antony.

There should be here, simultaneously with the movement of the hand, a forward inclination of the body—the natural expression of yielding.

3. For the sake of peace, I am willing to concede EVERY REASONABLE DEMAND.

4. I RELINQUISH any such expectation.

5. I WITHDRAW my motion.

6. I DECLINE the offer.

IV. Extreme Humility, Submission, Condescension, Obsequiousness.

Ex. — 1. I beg a THOUSAND PARDONS from your majesty.

2. Your very HUMBLE SERVANT, sir.

3.   Must I stand
  And CROUCH beneath your testy humor.
                      sus.

4.   Thanks to God
  For such a ROYAL LADY.

V. Privation, Destitution, Diminution, Nonentity.

Ex. — 1. They were but a FEEBLE band.

2. Merit like *his*, the fortune of the *mind*, BEGGARS all wealth.
   h. o.   imp.   d. l.   sus.

3. An *empire* thou couldst *crush, command, rebuild*,
   b. h. h. l.   b. h. d. o. p. b. h. h. o.   b. h. d. o.
   But govern not thy PETTIEST PASSION.
                                d. l.

4. They tell us, sir, that we are WEAK,

5. Shall we gather strength by IRRESOLUTION AND INACTION?

6. The army was reduced to utter DESTITUTION.

7. He was deprived of EVERY ADVANTAGE.

8. Treasures of wickedness PROFIT NOTHING.

9. Who steals my *purse*, steals TRASH.
   h. o.   d. l.

10. The *wine of life is drawn*, and the MERE LEES
    h. l.   d. l.
    Is left, this vault to brag of.   ·
    drop.

11. But *yesterday*, the word of Cæsar might
    h. o.
    Have stood against the *world;* now lies he *there*,
                          h. l.   d. o. ind.
    And NONE SO POOR to do him reverence.
    d. l.   sus.

12.   Thy joys
    Are placed in TRIFLES, FASHIONS, FOLLIES, TOYS.

et the hand move slowly through the series.

13.   All that *tread*
    The globe are but a HANDFULL to the tribes
    h. l.   d. l.
    That *slumber in its bosom.*
                  b. h. d. o. p.

VI. Abasement, Debasement, and kindred ideas.

.—1. For I know that in me, (that is, in my flesh,) dwelleth
    NO GOOD THING.

2. The inebriate descends to the level of the BRUTE.

3.   Minds,
    By *nature* great, are *conscious* of their greatness,
    h. o.   d. o.
    And hold it MEAN to borrow ought from FLATTERY.
    d. l.   imp.

4.   *Real* glory
        a. o.
Springs from the silent conquest of *ourselves*,
                   b. h. d. o.
And without that, the conqueror is nought
But the first SLAVE.
    d. l.

5. A courtier's dependent is a BEGGAR'S DOG.

6. The Lord bringeth the counsel of the heathen to NOUGHT.

VII. Scorn, Derision, Mockery, Contempt, Detestation, etc.

Ex.— 1. Thou makest us a *reproach* to our neighbors, a scorn and
                h. l.
    DERISION to them that are round about us.
    d. l.

2. O, when I am safe in my *sylvan home*,
               h. o.
   I MOCK at the pride of Greece and Rome.
   d. l.

VIII. Hopelessness, Extremity.

Ex.— 1. There is no HOPE of success.

2. It were utterly USELESS to resist.

3. It is in VAIN, sir, to extenuate the matter.

4. It is now TOO LATE to retire from the contest.

5. Delay is *bad*, doubt *worse*, desponding WORST.
    d. f.   d. o.   d. l.

6. Life *ill-preserved*, is WORSE THAN BADLY LOST.
    h. o.   d. l.

7. Love can *hope*, where reason would DESPAIR.
    a. f.   d. l.

8. He has gone to his rest—gone, to return NO MORE.

Right Hand Descending Oblique Backwards, Supine.

(FIG. 13.)

I. Emphatic or Vehement Rejection.

Ex.—AWAY with an idea so abhorrent to humanity!

II. Sometimes employed in Negation, and for other purposes usually assigned to the descending lateral,— to complete a series, to effect a climax, or to express greater degree.

Ex.—1. Let *another* man praise thee, and *not*
　　　　　h. o.　　　　　　　　　　　　h. l.
thine own mouth ; a stranger, and NOT
　h. o. b.　　　　d.o.b.
THINE OWN LIPS.

2. There is no *work*, nor *device*, nor *knowl-*
　　　　　　　d. f.　　　　d. o.　　　　d. l.
edge, nor WISDOM, in the GRAVE,
　　　　d. o. b.　　　　　　　　imp.
whither thou goest.

FIG. 13.

Right Hand Horizontal Front, Supine.
(FIG. 14.)

I. Direct Personal Address — Appeal, Challenge, Command, Exhortation, Interrogation, etc., etc.

Ex.—1. I appeal to YOU, sir, for the decision.

2. I challenge INVESTIGATION.

3. Give me good PROOFS of what you have alleged.

4. CHARGE ! Chester, CHARGE ! ON !
　r.h.h.f.　　　　　　　　　rep.　　r.h.h.f.
Stanley, ON !
　rep.

The fourth example requires an energetic forward motion of the body, and a corresponding fullness in the arm movement, the effect being quite different from that shown in the cut.

5.　　　　　　　　　Stand
FIRM for your country, and become a MAN,
　h. f.　　　　　　　　　　　　rep.
Honor'd and LOV'D.
　rep.

FIG. 14.

6. I court others in *verse*, but love thee in PROSE.
    h. l.   h. f.

They have my *whimsies*, but thou hast my HEART.
    h. l.   h. f.

7. THIS, above all, to thine own SELF be true.
    h. f.   rep.

8. Whatsoever thy hand FINDETH to do, do it with thy *might*.
              h. f.   d. f.

9. Know THYSELF.

10. Think for THYSELF ONE good idea,
        h. f.   rep.
   But known to be thine OWN,
             rep.
  Is better than a *thousand* gleaned
             h. l.
   From fields by *others* sown.
        imp.

11. Do you CONFESS the bond?

12. And why beholdest thou the *mote* that is in thy *brother's* eye,
                    h. l.   imp.
   but considerest not the BEAM that is in thine OWN eye?
            h. f.   imp.

II. Unemphatic Particular Assertion.

Ex.—LIVING I shall assert it, *dying* I shall assert it.
   h. f.   d. f.

Here we have the unemphatic as compared with the emphatic.

III. Presentation. This may refer to visible objects, or to time, space, or thought.

Ex. — 1. With THIS HAND I signed the pledge.

2. The world at this MOMENT is regarding us with a *willing*, but
             h. f.   h. o.
  something of a *fearful* admiration.
           d. o.
  THIS is the place, the CENTER of the grove.
   h. f.   rep.

3. THIS is the proposition to be discussed.

4. Did THIS in Cæsar seem AMBITIOUS?
    h. f.   imp.

5. The Jews require a *sign*, and the Greeks seek after *wisdom;* but
             h. l.   h. o. b.
  we preach Christ CRUCIFIED.
        h. f.

The ideas of the Jews and Greeks are rejected, **and** something else presented instead; hence the contrast in gesture—presentation as opposed to rejection; not *that*, but *this*.

h. l.   h. f.

IV. Directness, Boldness, Integrity.

Ex.—1. True as the STEEL of their tried blades.

    2. I speak the TRUTH, the WHOLE truth, and nothing *but* the

       truth.   h. f.   imp.   d. f.

For emphatic distinction, the action here, as in many similar cases, is consummated in the descending line.

    3. Was it *ambition* that induced Regulus to return to Carthage?

       h. o.

       No; but a love of *country* and respect for TRUTH—an act of

       d. o.   h. l.   h. f.

       moral *sublimity* arising out of the firmest INTEGRITY.

       a. o.   h. f.

V. Impulsion, Forward Motion.

Ex.—1. True eloquence urges the whole man ONWARD, right ONWARD

       to his object.   h. f.   rep. with

                                         larger prep.

    2. ON, Comrades, ON!

       h. f.   rep.

    3. FORWARD, the Light Brigade!

The coincidence of this with a preceding application —that of command—renders the action doubly expressive.

VI. Futurity.

Ex.—1. The future lies BEFORE us.

    2. Anticipation FORWARD points the view.

Right Hand Horizontal Oblique Supine.
(FIG. 15.)

I. General Address, as distinguished from particular personal address, which takes the line in front; Presentation, etc.

Ex.—1. Conscript FATHERS, I do not rise to
 h. o.
waste the night in *words.*
 h. l.

2. Fellow-citizens, I CONGRATULATE you on the return of this anniversary.

3. For the truth of my statement, I appeal to THESE WITNESSES.

4. THESE are my sentiments, gentlemen.

5. I now submit these questions to YOU, my friends.

6. SPEAK the speech, I pray you, as I PRO-
 h. o.   imp.
NOUNCED it to you.

FIG. 15.

II. General Reference as distinguished from particular personal reference; Respectful Reference.

Ex.—1. For the *justice* of this principle, I refer you to the decisions of
 h. f.
the COURTS.
 h. o.

2. Then must the Jew be MERCIFUL.

The grammatical *third person singular* is embraced in the term *general* as employed in this treatise. If Portia were using the form of the *second person*—Then must thou be merciful, Shylock—this direct personal address would call for the gesture in front. This rule, however, is by no means invariable, as may be seen from many of the examples given elsewhere. Gesture inclines to the line *in front* by the law of emphasis alone, regardless of every other law. In many other cases, also, as in classification, comparison and contrast, it is found convenient to make exceptions to the rule.

> 3. I acknowledge my sincere REGARD for the honorable gentleman who preceded me.

III. Unemphatic General Assertion, or Expression of General Thought. Appropriate in Interrogation, etc.

Ex.—1. Man is MORTAL.
   2. All men are created EQUAL.
   3. What was the OBJECT of his ambition?
   4. Who knows the joys of FRIENDSHIP?

The attention of the student is here called to the prominence which should be given to the present gesture—horizontal oblique—together with the descending oblique, in *general assertion*. Sentences may often be treated as mere assertions, even though they contain some word suggestive of a descriptive or designative gesture.

In particular, and very emphatic assertion, as previously shown, the corresponding front lines are preferred, and these four gestures, although employed for various other purposes, may, by way of distinction, be called assertive gestures, and classified as follows:

Horizontal front, unemphatic particular assertion;
Horizontal oblique, unemphatic general assertion;
Descending front, emphatic particular assertion;
Descending oblique, emphatic general assertion.

In didactic and argumentative discourse, these gestures predominate. However, as the delivery becomes more emotional or impassioned, the left hand will be brought in as an accompaniment to the right, as will be shown under *both hands supine*.

IV. Closely allied to the preceding designation, we have for this gesture the Suspension of Thought. The horizontal oblique is thus employed in connection with some other gesture which is added to continue or to complete the expression.

Ex.—1. Before REINFORCEMENTS could be sent, the battle was *lost*.
            h. o.   d. o.

  2. The steed at HAND, why *longer* tarry?
             h o.   d. o.

  3. That RICHES are to be preferred to WISDOM, no one will *openly*
          h. o.   imp.   d. o.
     assert.

  4. The brave man will CONQUER, or *perish* in the attempt.
          h. o.   d. o.

  5. To SMILE upon those we should CENSURE, and to *countenance*
     h. o.   imp.   h. l.
     such as are guilty of *bad* actions, is bringing guilt upon *our-*
                     imp.   d. o.
     selves.

Antithesis and Comparison properly fall under this head. To illustrate these the examples are continued:

  6. The prodigal robs his HEIR; the miser robs *himself*.
          h. o.   d. o.

  7. He that cannot BEAR a jest, should not *make* one.
         h. o.   d. o.

  8. All who have been great and good WITHOUT Christianity, would
                           h. o.
     have been much greater and better *with* it.
                     d. o.

Also Hypothetical Clauses:

  9. If the war be CONTINUED, the public treasury will be *exhausted*,
          h. o.   d. o.

 10. If sheep and OXEN could atone for men,
    prep.   h. o.
     Ah! at how cheap a rate the *rich* might sin!
    r.h. upl.   d. o.

Other gestures are sometimes brought in to extend the suspension of thought; as,

4

11. If ONE man can do much good, if TWO can do more, and if three
h. f.   h. o.
can go FAR BEYOND two; what may we not expect *three*
h. l.
hundred thousand to accomplish?
b. h. h. l.

12. Whatever tends to promote the principles of VIRTUE, and
h. f.
strengthen the bonds of BROTHERHOOD—whatever tends to
h. o.
CALM THE RUFFLED FEELINGS and REGULATE THE PASSIONS,
h. o. p.   h. l. p.
is undoubtedly a source of *happiness.*
d. o.

To this head may also be referred those cases in which the subject of an unimpassioned sentence occurs upon the horizontal oblique, the predicate usually taking an emphatic downward stroke:

13. The LOVE OF MONEY is the root of *all evil.*
h. o.   d. o.

14. TYRANTS, when reason and ARGUMENT make against them, have
h. o.   rep.
recourse to *violence* to silence their opponents.
d. o.

15. NATIONS, as well as MEN, fail in nothing which they *boldly*
h. o.   imp.   d. o.
undertake.

It will be observed that much prominence is given to the gesture horizontal oblique supine. This and the corresponding gesture in the descending line are more frequently employed than any others in this system.

Right Hand Horizontal Lateral Supine.

(FIG. 16.)

For the full effect of the curve, the movements terminating in the lateral positions—descending, horizontal and ascending—are made with a full sweep of the hand, which is first carried to the corresponding oblique line, and thence outward to the lateral, thus: for the descending lateral, first make the descending oblique (omitting the emphatic stroke at its terminus), and then carry the hand around to the descending lateral; for the horizontal lateral, give the horizontal oblique, and sweep outward thence to the horizontal lateral; for the ascending lateral, move to the ascending oblique, and continue the action to the ascending lateral; carefully avoiding, in each case, the *angle* which would be formed by allowing the hand to pause at the oblique extremity,

FIG. 16.

and making the motions continuous and curvilineal. The close observance of these directions will prove an effectual safeguard against the prevalent fault of divesting this class of gestures of their gracefulness and expressive power.

In the interpretation of this gesture we have,

I. Extension in time and space, and, by analogy, extension in thought.

Allusion to numbers and space frequently uses this in preference to the corresponding gesture with both hands.

Ex.—1. From infancy TO OLD AGE.

    2. DAYS, MONTHS, YEARS AND AGES shall circle away.
Slow movement extending through the series.   sus.

    3. From the center ALL AROUND TO THE SEA, I am lord of the fowl and the brute.

4. His capacious mind RANGED OVER THE WHOLE SUBJECT.

5. Shall TRIBULATION, OR DISTRESS, OR PERSECUTION, OR FAMINE, OR NAKEDNESS, OR PERIL, OR SWORD?

Slow movement throughout. This takes the supine on account of its interrogatory character. Tribulation, distress, etc., in themselves considered, would require the prone hand. The terms here employed, though numerous and descriptive, are merged in a sweeping unity of effect; so of the gesture.

6. Where is the *wise?* Where is the *scribe?* Where is the DISPUTER
         h. f.   h. o.   h. l.
   OF THIS WORLD?

Here the lateral gesture is brought in to complete the series. The thought may be extended either by one sweeping gesture, as in Ex. 5, or by using the lateral in connection with the front and oblique, as in Ex. 6.

7. The morning was pure and *sunny*, the fields were white with
                              h. f.

   daisies, and BEES HUMMED ABOUT EVERY BANK.
    h. o.   h. l.

8. A proverb is the *wit of one*, and the WISDOM OF MANY.
                      h. o.   h. l.

II. Descriptive Reference. While objects may be descriptively referred to with any other gesture, the *horizontal latéral*, because of its greater prominence in this respect, is worthy of special notice.

Ex.—1. The breeze of morning WAFTED INCENSE ON THE AIR.

2. O'ER THE RIVER, THE VILLAGE, THE FIELD, AND THE WOOD.

This requires a full preparation, and large outward sweep. Nor must the hand be allowed to pause with the rhetorical pauses in the voice.

III. Disclosing, Revealing, Showing, Displaying, etc.

Ex.—1. His faults LIE OPEN TO THE LAWS.

2. O, what a GOODLY OUTSIDE falsehood hath !

3. Professing themselves to be WISE, they became *fools*.
   h. l.   d. l.

4. This world is all a FLEETING SHOW.
   h. l.

In the last example the gesture expresses a complex idea—transition and display.

IV. Distant Reference—distance in time or space.

Ex.—1. Methinks I saw thee STRAYING ON THE BEACH.

2. The brave ABROAD fight for the wise at *home*.
   h. l.   h. f.

3. Our ABSENT friends are remembered in these festive seasons.

4. Search the records of our EARLY HISTORY for a parallel to this.

5. The blessed *to-day* are as *completely* so
   h. f.   d. o.
   As who began THREE THOUSAND YEARS AGO.
                                    h. l.

V. Removal, Withdrawal, Transition, etc.

This being the gesture of *distance*—distance in a greater or less degree—it is often used in referring to *that* and *those*, as distinguished from *this* and *these*, which incline to the front and oblique. *Here* and *there* follow the same law.

Frequently used in connection with the horizontal front, or, it may be, some other gesture, to express Antithesis, or Parallelism.

Ex.—1. The objection to this measure is now REMOVED.

2. Go, say I SENT THEE FORTH to purchase HONOR.
                                        imp.

3. Through floods and through forests he BOUNDED AWAY.

4. *Man* may DISMISS COMPASSION from his heart,
   h. o.   sus.
   But God will *never*.
             d. o.

5.   His cares FLEW AWAY,
                          h. l.

And visions of *happiness* danced o'er his mind.
                    a. o.

6. He WITHDREW from the cares of the world.

7. The fashion of this world PASSETH AWAY.

8. The man that wandereth out of the way of UNDERSTANDING,
     shall remain in the congregation of the *dead*.   h. l.
                                          d. l.

9. And of Zion it shall be said, *This* and THAT man was born in
     her.   h. f.   h. l.

10. Some place the bliss in ACTION, some in *ease* —
                            h. l.   h. o.

Those call it PLEASURE, and *contentment* these.
              h. l.   h. o.

11. Call imperfection what thou *fancy'st* such,
                              h. o.

Say, *here* he gives too *little*, THERE too MUCH.
    h. f.   imp.   h. l.   imp.

12. The *wise* man is happy when he gains his *own* approbation, the
      h. f.   imp.

FOOL when he gains that of OTHERS.
h. l.   imp.

13. A man's *first* care should be to avoid the reproaches of his *own*
            h. f.   imp.

heart; his next, to escape the censure of the WORLD.
                                              h. l.

14. When our vices LEAVE US, we flatter ourselves *we leave them.*
                    h. l.   d. l.

15. The wicked FLEE WHEN NO MAN PURSUETH: but the righteous .
                h. l.

are bold as a *lion.*
              d. o.

VI. Unemphatic Negation.

This comes from the primary idea of removal. To deny a proposition is to remove it from the mind. "We posite by an affirmative; we remove by a negative."

Ex.—1. Galio cared for NONE of these things.

2 Cæsar was not more ambitious than CICERO.

3. We shall not fight our battles ALONE.

That is, Galio dismissed the whole affair from his thoughts; we remove from our minds the proposition that Cæsar was more ambitious than Cicero; we put away the discouraging thought of fighting our battles alone : hence the gesture of removal.

    4. I have not STOPPED MINE EARS to their demands.

    5. Angels, *contented* with their fame in *Heaven*, seek not the praise
       of MEN.   a. o.   imp.
       h. l.

(*Negation as opposed to affirmation.*)

    6. Not that I loved Cæsar LESS, but that I loved Rome *more.*
             h. l.   d. o.

    7. You were paid to *fight* against Alexander, not to RAIL at him.
                d. o.   h. l.

    8. *True politeness* is not a mere compliance with arbitrary CUSTOM,
        h. o.   h. l.
      it is the expression of a refined *benevolence.*
                        d. o.

What may be termed the weak negative, in contrast with the strong negative, may be expressed by a moderate upward, downward, or horizontal wave, according to its degree of sublimity, energy, or moderation.

VII. Remission.

Ex.—I freely FORGIVE you.

The same language uttered with greater emphasis would take the descending lateral ; and if accompanied with strong emotion, both hands.

VIII. Concession, in a moderate degree.

Ex -1. I acknowledge his greatness as a MILITARY LEADER, but I doubt
      the *sincerity* of his intentions.   h. l.
      d. l.

    2. Others may be WISER, but none are more *amiable.*
        h. l.   d. o.

    3. The *miracles* that Moses performed may have CONVINCED
        h. o.   h. l.
      Pharaoh, but at first they humbled not his *pride.*
                               d. o.

4. He who lacks *decision of character*, may win the LOVE, but he
          h. o.   h. l.
certainly cannot gain the *respect* of his fellow-men.
                                  d. o.

IX. Disregard, Diminution, Humor, Derision, Ridicule, Mockery, Irony, Sarcasm, etc., when unemphatic.
When emphatic they take the descending line.

This is the gesture of slighting, rather than of con-
temning. The latter usually prefers the descending
line.

The lateral gesture indicates breadth; and rhetoricians
speak of the "breadth of humor."

In derision, ridicule, etc., we remove, or set aside,
whatever is inconsistent with reason; hence we employ
the gesture of Removal.

Ex.—1. I have very little REGARD for such assertions.

    2. The gay will LAUGH when thou art gone.

    3. MERRY is the bird's life, in the pleasant spring !
                                            sus.

    4. Full WELL they laughed with COUNTERFEITED glee.
        h. l.   imp.

    5. Let the *fools* who follow fortune live upon her SMILES.
           h. o.   h. l.

    6. Dreams are the children of an IDLE BRAIN.
       Begot of nothing but *fantasy*.   h. l.
                        d. l.

    7. And what is friendship but a NAME,
       A charm that lulls to *sleep*. h. l.
                  d. l.

    8. Fools are only LAUGHED at—wits are *hated*.
         h. l.   d. l.

    9. What fairer cloak than COURTESY for fraud?

  10. What is *ambition?*   'T is a glorious CHEAT.
        h. o.   h. l.

  11. COURAGEOUS chief!   The FIRST in flight from pain

  12. It has been said that this law is a measure of *peace!*   Yes! such
      peace as the WOLF gives to the LAMB !   h. o.
      h. l.

Right Hand Horizontal Oblique Backwards Supine.

(FIG. 17.)

I. Remote Reference—remoteness in time or space.

It will be observed that this completes the series,—horizontal front, *personal* reference; horizontal oblique, *general* reference; horizontal lateral, *distant* reference; horizontal oblique backwards, *remote* reference.

These several relations may also be stated thus: h. f., *present;* h. o., *near;* h. l., *distant;* h. o. b., *remote.*

FIG. 17.

Ex.—1. Turning his back upon country, kith and kin, he wandered FAR AWAY TO FOREIGN LANDS.

2.   TRADITION'S pages
Tell not the planting of the parent tree.

3. Search the records of the remotest ANTIQUITY for a parallel to this.

4.   The ashes of my ANCESTORS,
           h. o. b.
If intermingled in the tomb with *kings,*
           b. h. d. f.
Could hardly be distinguished.
.drop.

II. Retrogression.

Ex.—The children of *Ephraim,* being armed, and carrying *bows,* TURNED
       h. o.   imp.   h. o. b.
BACK in the day of battle.

In addition to the applications here given, the gestures oblique backwards, in the descending, the horizontal, and the ascending lines, are sometimes used in connection with the corresponding lateral gestures merely to complete a series, or to express greater degree.

4*

Right Hand Ascending Front Supine.
(FIG. 18.)

FIG. 18.

I. Elevation — physical, intellectual, or moral; Sacredness, Sublimity, Sublime Apostrophe.

Ex.—1. Climb to the MOUNTAIN TOP.

2. Aspire to the HIGHEST and NOBLEST attainments.

The superlative degree usually prefers the line in front.

3. Wisdom sits ALONE,
   TOPMOST in heaven,
   rep.

4. Thou SUN! of this great world both eye and SOUL!

II. Sacred Address.

Ex.—1. Thou art MY FATHER.

2. I appeal to the great SEARCHER OF HEARTS for the truth of what I utter.

III. Sacred Reference—Direct Reference to God, or His throne.

Ex.—1. 'T was GOD who fixed the rolling spheres.

2. The throne of ETERNITY is a throne of mercy and LOVE.

IV. Futurity, Sublime Anticipation.

The future as related to time, when not associated with sublimity, usually employs the horizontal gesture: the future as related to eternity—a blissful eternity—the ascending.

Ex.—1. For EVER shall His throne endure.

If, in this case, it should suit the purpose of the speaker to emphasize the assertion rather than to employ a gesture suggestive of futurity, he would of course choose the downward, instead of the upward motion, simply treating the sentence as an emphatic assertion.

> 2. On *Jordan's* stormy banks I stand,
> h. f.
> And cast a *wishful* eye
> The eyes upraised.
> To CANAAN's fair and happy land,
> a. f.
> Where my *possessions* lie.
> b. h. a. o.

> 3. O, holy Star of HOPE!
> a. f.

The objects of hope lying above and beyond us, suggest this gesture in the present case.

Right Hand Ascending Oblique Supine.

(FIG. 19.)

I. General Sublimity.

Ex.—1. Day gilds the MOUNTAIN TOPS.

2. Aspire after the rewards of a truly NOBLE ambition.

3. *Hark!* the herald ANGELS sing.
r. h. upl.   a. o.

II. General Sacred Reference.

Ex.—The Scriptures represent God as the Father of ALL MERCIES.

FIG. 19.

Right Hand Ascending Lateral Supine.
(Fig. 20.)

Fig. 20.

I. Elevation, Sacredness, or Sublimity, combined with Extension or Distance.

Since the ascending gestures express elevation, sacredness and sublimity, and the lateral indicate extension and distance, the ascending lateral gives this combination.

Ex.—1. From star to STAR thy glory
prep.
shines.
sus.

2. And mountain top to DISTANT
prep.
mountain top REPEATS the
sounding joy.

II. Descriptive Reference combined with Elevation or Sublimity, Sublime Classification, and Enumeration.

Ex.—The *sun*, the *moon*, the STARS His majesty proclaim.
a. f.   a. o.   a. l.   sus.

Or, the whole may be embraced in one sweep of the hand, terminating in the ascending lateral.

III. Victory, Triumph, Exultation.

Ex.—1. In dreams his song of TRIUMPH heard.

2. His few surviving comrades saw
His *smile* when rang their proud HURRAH!
h. o.   a. l.

Right Hand Ascending Oblique Backwards Supine.
(FIG. 21.)

I. Remoteness in time or space, associated with Elevation or Sublimity.

Ex.—1. This glorious scheme was projected from the foundation of the WORLD.

    2. You *may*, if it be God's will, gain our
       h. o.
    barren and rugged *mountains;* but,
         a. l.
    like our *ancestors* of old, we will
        h. o. b.
    take refuge in WILDER and more
        a. o. b.
    DISTANT solitudes.
    rep.

FIG. 21.

II. Victory, Triumph, Exultation, the arm making a wider sweep than in the lateral, to express a higher degree of exultation, or to effect a climax.

Ex.—1. Shout, shout ALOUD for joy!

    2. We shall come off *conquerors*, and MORE than conquerors.
        a. l.   a. o. b.

CHAPTER V.

BOTH HANDS SUPINE.

Both hands are employed to indicate space and numbers. The latter is based upon the geometrical idea of representing numbers by space. By analogy we use both hands to express the expansion of thought and feeling. They do not, as many young speakers suppose, add emphasis; but give to the expression warmth, expansion, or entireness. Their too frequent use is a fault, tending to weaken the action.

Genial and joyous emotions frequently require both hands.

EXAMPLE.—O, the transporting RAPTUROUS scene
          b. h. a. f.
     That rises to my sight,

     Sweet fields arrayed in LIVING GREEN,
          b. h. a. l.
     And rivers of DELIGHT.
          b. h. a. o.

To express the joyousness of this language, one hand would be too sparing.

In Impassioned Discourse we have the union of force and feeling—Impassioned Emphasis—which calls for both hands; unimpasssioned emphasis requiring only one hand. The right hand is the symbol of authority and power; hence it is adapted to accompany forcible utterance.

Both Hands Descending Front Supine.
(FIG. 22.)

I. Impassioned Particular Assertion, whether affirmative or negative.

Ex.—1. This principle is as firm as the solid ROCK.

    2. The assertion of my opponent is utterly FALSE.

    3. Give me *liberty*, or give me DEATH.
       b. h. a. o.   b. h. d. f.

II. Deposition, Surrender, etc.

Ex.—1.   We will resign
    Thy sacred dust to EARTH'S cold breast.

The student will observe that the gesture, as applied to this example, is intended to describe the act of deposit-
FIG. 22.
ing the body, rather than the subsequent idea of its being covered beneath the earth; hence the hands are supine instead of prone.

    2. All *personal* feeling he deposited upon the altar of his COUNRTY.
     b. h. h. f.   b. h. d. f.

In partial deposition, or surrender, the arms are bent at the elbows; to produce the fullest effect they should be straight. In proportion as we bend the arms we withhold the offering. The arm is a tongue that speaks what is in the soul, full or feeble.

III. Humility, Submission.

These are expressed in different degrees, according as the body is more or less inclined forward.

Ex.—1. (*First degree.*) I SUBMIT.

    2. (*Second degree.*) I RESPECTFULLY submit.

    3. (*Third degree.*) I HUMBLY submit.

    4. Here I stand your SLAVE.

5.   Here I KNEEL :
    If e'er my will did trespass 'gainst his love,
    Either in discourse, or thought, or actual deed.

IV. Depth or Descent.

Ex.—1. Errors, like straws, upon the *surface* flow ;
                                     h. o. p.
    He who would search for pearls, must dive BELOW.
                                              b. h. d. f.

2. DEEP calleth unto DEEP at the noise of thy water spouts.

3. Thou hast laid me in the LOWEST PIT.

4. Yea, though I pass through the Valley of the Shadow of DEATH, I
    will fear no evil.

5. O DEATH, where is thy sting ?

6. A fire is kindled in mine anger, and shall burn unto the LOWEST
    HELL.

7. Into the mouth of HELL rode the six hundred.

8. They spend their days in *wealth*, and in a moment go down to
    the GRAVE.   b. h. h. o.
       b. h. d. f.

References like these, tending to narrow and confine
the action, naturally employ this gesture.

Both Hands Descending Oblique Supine.
(FIG. 23.)

I. Emphatic assertion in connection
with numbers, or space.

Ex.—1. The mind doth shape itself to its own
        wants, and can bear ALL THINGS.
        b. h. h. f.   b. h. d. o.

This notation must be considered
with reference to the emphasis rather
than to the descriptive effect; otherwise, *all things* would take b. h. h. l.

2. Yet *millions* never think a NOBLE thought.
    b. h. h. o.   b. h. d. o.

By the law of analogy, reference
to *noble thoughts*, as such, would re-

FIG. 23.

quire the ascending gesture, but in the present case the emphatic negation takes precedence, and employs the descending line.

II. Impassioned General Assertion, whether affirmative or negative.

Ex.—1. These are the WORST of abuses.

    2. These allegations are utterly UNTRUE.

III. Consummation and Finalty.

When thus employed—for completeness of effect—this gesture may also coincide with either of the preceding applications; that is to say, the expression may be consummated in an emphatic assertion associated with numbers or space, or in an impassioned emphatic general assertion; or there may be a coincidence of all three.

Ex.—1. Let the *sea* roar, and the *fulness* thereof; the *world*, and they
       b. h. h. o.   b. h. h. l.   b. h. h. o.
      that DWELL therein.
      b. h. d. o.

    2. Without *counsel*, purposes are *disappointed*; but in the *multitude*
          h. o.   d. o.   b. h. h. o.
      of counsellors they are ESTABLISHED.
      b. h. d. o.

    3. His terrors keep the world in *awe;*
          r. h. h. o. p.
      His justice guards his holy *law;*
          r. h. h. l. p.
      His love reveals a *smiling face;*
          b. h. h. o.
      His truth and promise SEAL the grace.
      b. h. d. o.

IV. General Deposition, or Surrender.

Ex.—1. We commit these bodies to the EARTH.

    2. Every *personal* advantage he surrendered to the COMMON good.
      b h. h. o.   b. h. d. o.

V. Concession.

Ex.—We CONCEDE these points.

VI. Humility, General Submission.

Ex.—1. We humbly CONFESS our faults.

   2.   It grieves me to the soul
To see how man SUBMITS TO MAN'S CONTROL.

To express humility, the hands should descend lower than in the ordinary descending gesture.   There should also be a corresponding inclination of the body forward.

Both Hands Descending Lateral Supine.

(FIG. 24.)

In the execution of this gesture avoid keeping the elbows too near the body—a posture suited only to comedy.

FIG. 24.

I. Depth and Extent combined.   Expansion, Separation.

Ex.—1. The dread *volcano* ministers
                              d. o.
          good.
          h. l.
          Its smothered flames might
          undermine the WORLD.
                              b. h. d. l.

   2. WIDE is the gate and BROAD
      b. h. d. l.   rep.
          is the way that leadeth to
          DESTRUCTION.
          imp.

   3. And there were sudden PART-
                              b. h. d. l.
      INGS, such as press
      The *life* from out young hearts.
      b. h. d. f.

II. Descent, combined with numbers or space ; hence, Abundance, Fullness, Completeness.   Descending streams of Divine goodness prompt this gesture.

Ex.—1. Here pardon, life and joy *divine*,
                              b. h. a. o.
      In rich PROFUSION flow.
      b. h. d. l.

2. Bring ye all the tithes into the *storehouse*, that there may be
　　　　　　　　　　　　　　　　　b. h. h. f.

　　meat in mine house, and *prove* me now herewith, saith the
　　imp.　　　　　　　　　　　rep.

　　Lord of hosts, if I will not open you the windows of *heaven*
　　　　　　　　　　　　　　　　　　　　　　　　b. h. a. o.

　　and pour you out a blessing, that there shall not be ROOM
　　　　　　　　　　　　　　　　　　　　　　　b. h. d. l.

　　ENOUGH TO RECEIVE IT.

III. Removal. So employed in impassioned discourse, and in connection with numbers or space.

Ex.—1. Every obstacle to this measure is for ever SWEPT AWAY.

　　2. All the foundations of the earth are OUT OF COURSE.

IV. Remission, in the fullest degree.

Ex.—And sinners plunged beneath *that* flood,
　　　　　　　　　　　　　　b. h. d. o.

　　LOSE ALL THEIR GUILTY STAINS.
　　b. h. d. l.

V. Concession in the fullest degree.

Ex.—I concede EVERY POINT claimed in the argument.

VI. Submission, Extreme Humility.

Ex.—1. I submit myself ENTIRELY TO YOUR DISPOSAL.

　　2. Ye *worlds* and every living *thing*,
　　　b. h. a. o.　　　　　　　b. h. a. l.
　　　Fulfill his high command ;
　　　b. h. h. o.
　　　Pay grateful *homage* to your king,
　　　　　b. h. d. o.
　　　And OWN HIS RULING HAND.
　　　　b. h. d. l.

VII. Absolute Renunciation, Relinquishment, Utter Abandonment, Hopelessness. The gesture of extremity.

Ex.—1. I utterly RENOUNCE all the supposed advantages of such a station.
　　　　　　　　　　　　　　　　　　　　　　　　　　　　sus

　　2. 　　　　　O, you mighty *gods!*
　　　　　　　　　　b. h. a. o.
　　　This world I do RENOUNCE ; and in your sight,
　　　　　　b. h. d. l.
　　　Shake patiently my great affliction OFF.
　　　　　　　　　　　　　　　rep

　　3. I utterly RELINQUISH any such expectation.

The philosophy of this notation will appear by a comparison of the last example above with the following:
I do most fondly CHERISH these expectations.
b. h. h. f.

    4. If thou dost *slander her* and *torture me,*
        r. h. h. f. ind.   rep.

       Never *pray more;* ABANDON ALL REMORSE.
         rep.   b. h. d. l.

    5. How *unsearchable* are His judgments, and His ways PAST FINDING
       OUT. b. h. d. f.   b. h. d. l.

The impossibility of finding out the ways of the Infinite suggests here the gesture of hopelessness.

    6. Plunged in a gulf of dark *despair,*
        b. h. d. f.

       We wretched sinners lay,

       Without one cheerful beam of HOPE,
                b. h. d. l.

       Or SPARK of glimmering day.
       imp.

    7. All is LOST !

Under a high state of excitement, despair would be more fully expressed with the hands prone, or with the clinched hands, or, in extreme cases, pressed upon the forehead.

VIII. Privation, Destitution, Diminution, etc.

Ex.—1.   All, when life is *new,*
            r. h. h. o.

       Commence with feelings *warm,* and prospects *high,*
            b. h. h. o   b. h. a. o.

       But time STRIPS our illusions of their hue.
       b. h. d. l.

    2. This cruel war has reduced the nation to BANKRUPTCY.

    3. All this boasted knowledge of the *world,*
            b. h. h. o.

       To me seems but to mean acquaintance with

       Low things, or evil, or INDIFFERENT.
       b. h. d. f.   prep.   b. h. d. l.

    4. Look how we *grovel* here below,
        b. h. d. f.

       Fond of these TRIFLING TOYS.
          b. h. d. l.

5. I have seen all the works that are under the *sun*, and behold all
is VANITY and vexation of SPIRIT.   b. h. h. l.
    b. h. d. l.   rep.

IX. Cessation, Destruction, Annihilation, Non-existence.

Ex.—1. This vast and solid *earth*, that blazing *sun*,
    b. h. h. l.   a. f. ind.

Those *skies* through which it rolls must all have END.
    b. h. a. o.   b. h. d. l.

2.   Still, monarchs dream
Of universal *empire* growing up
    b. h. h. l.

From universal RUIN.
    b. h. d. l.

Accompanied with strong emotion, or under any circumstances calling for a purely descriptive effect, reference to universal ruin would require the prone hands.

3. He saw nothing around him but utter VACUITY.

Both Hands Horizontal Front Supine.
(FIG. 25.)

I. Earnest Entreaty.

Ex.—Listen, I IMPLORE you, to the voice of reason.

Earnest entreaty assumes an advanced position, inclining the body forward more or less, according to the degree of earnestness.

II. Bold Challenge.

Ex.—1. I challenge you to your PROOFS.

2.   COME, Rhoderic Dhu,
And of his clan the BOLDEST two.
If there be three in all your *company*, dare
                  r. h. h. o.

face me on the *bloody sands*, let them
COME ON.   r. h. h. l. ind.
b. h. h. f.

FIG. 25.

Bold challenge assumes a retired position, bracing the body for resistance. Neither Rhoderic Dhu nor the gladiators of Capua are here welcomed to a feast, but challenged to a fight. The distinction consists not so much in the notation of the gesture as in the manner of its execution, which affects the whole posture of the body.

3. Here I stand for *impeachment* or *trial!*   I *dare* accusation!   I
        h. f.   d. f.   h. f.

    DEFY the honorable gentleman!   I defy the *Government!*   I
    b. h. h. f.   b. h. h. o.

    defy the whole *phalanx!*   Let them come FORTH!
        b. h. h. l.   b. h. h. f.

III. Bold Command.

Ex.—1. Press bravely ONWARD!

2. ON! ON!—was still his stern exclaim.

On the repeated word the gesture should be repeated, with larger preparation and more force both of voice and action.

IV. Impulsion, Propulsion.

Ex.—1. ONWARD they march embattled, to the sound
     b. h. h. f.
Of martial *harmony.*
     b. h. a. o.

2. Then rushed the STEEDS to BATTLE driven.
                       imp.

3. Destruction rushes DREADFUL to the field,
            b. h. h. f.
And *bathes* itself in blood.
    b. h. d. f.

V. Contiguity—Applicable either to friendly meeting, or to hostile opposition.

Ex.—1. The rich and the poor MEET TOGETHER.

2. Mercy and truth are MET TOGETHER, righteousness and peace have KISSED each other.

3. The eager armies met to TRY their cause.

4.   Front to FRONT,
Bring thou this fiend of Scotland and myself.
                        sus.

5. When Greek MEETS Greek, then comes the TUG of war.

6. CONFRONT the battery's jaws of flame.

7. Wisdom and fortune COMBATTING together ;

b. h. h. f.

If that the former DARE but what it CAN,

rep.   rep.

No chance may *shake* it.

b. h. d. f.

VI. Presentation.

Ex.—1. THESE are the facts upon which I base my argument.

sus.

2, *Home, kindred, friends, and country*—THESE are ties with which

h. l.   b. h. h. f.

we *never* part.

b. h. d. f.

Here we first enumerate a series, sweeping through it with one hand in descriptive reference, and then, as it were, gather up and present the whole with both hands. For greater emphasis, as well as for completeness of effect, the action is finished in the descending line.

Both Hands Horizontal Oblique Supine.
(FIG. 26.)

The general tendency here to spread the hands too wide apart should be carefully avoided. Half way between the front and the lateral is the rule. Better a little inside, than outside of this line.

I. General Address — Appeal, Command, Exhortation, Welcome, etc.

Ex.—1. Fellow-citizens: I appeal to your better JUDGMENT for the decision of this question.

2. To ARMS! To ARMS! A thousand voices cried. rep.

FIG. 26.

3. ARM, warriors, ARM for the fight.

4. Come ON, then ; be MEN.

5. Come FORTH, O ye children of gladness, COME !

6. WELCOME once more to your early home !
sus.

7. Our hearts and our hands are open to RECEIVE you.

8. Friends, Romans, COUNTRYMEN, lend me your EARS.
　prep.　　　　　　　b. h. h. o.　　　　　　　rep.

II. Opening, Disclosing, Revealing, etc.

Ex.—1. In the last great day the books shall be OPENED.

2. The secret thoughts of our hearts shall be REVEALED.

3. His love reveals a SMILING FACE.

III. Fulness, Abundance, and, by analogy, genial and expansive ideas generally.

Ex.—1. The Lord fulfill ALL THY PETITIONS.

2. In the house of the righteous is much TREASURE.

3. The field of honorable labor lies BEFORE us.

4. This is my OWN, my NATIVE land.

5.　　　　　　　Mingles with the friendly *bowl,*
　　　　　　　　　　r. h. h. o.
The feast of REASON and the flow of SOUL.
　b. h. h. o.　　　　　　　　　rep.

6. The world is BRIGHT before thee.

7. Christianity breathes love and peace and good WILL to man.
　　　prep.

IV. Comparison and Contrast, Resemblance, Parallelism, etc.

Ex.—1. Take THESE THINGS and compare them.
　　　　　　　　　　sus.

2. In the day of prosperity be *joyful,* but in the day of adversity
　　　　　　　　　　　a. o.

consider : God also hath set the *one* over against the OTHER.
　h. f. ind.　　　　　　prep.　　　　　　b. h. h. o.

3. To Him the darkness and the light are both ALIKE.

4. Our Great Advocate is allied to BOTH parties in this controversy.

V. Forward Motion.　When less emphatic, or when

embracing more space, this frequently prefers the oblique to the front.

Ex.—1. ROLL ON, thou deep and dark blue ocean—ROLL.
rep.

2.   The eternal surge
Of time and tide ROLLS ON.

3. Life bears us on like the current of a MIGHTY RIVER.

4. ADVANCE, then, ye FUTURE generations.

Both Hands Horizontal Lateral Supine.

(FIG. 27.)

FIG. 27.

I. Large Numbers or Space, Universality, Utmost Expansion, Universal Appeal, Challenge, etc.

Ex.—1. Is not the king's name FORTY THOUSAND names?

2. They yet slept in the WIDE ABYSS OF POSSIBILITY.

3. How many pleasant faces shed their light on EVERY SIDE.

4. Let the *sea* roar, and the
b. h. h. o.
FULNESS thereof.
b. h. h. l.

5. Knowledge or wealth to few are given,
r. h. h. l.
But mark how *just* the ways of Heaven:
h. o. ind.
True joy to ALL is free.
b. h. h. l.

6. These glorious truths shall be diffused throughout the WHOLE WORLD.

7. All the ends of the EARTH have seen the salvation of our God.

8. Let every thing that hath BREATH praise the Lord.

9. I appeal to the impartial judgment of ALL MANKIND.

10. Come one, come ALL ! this *rock* shall fly
       b. h. h. l.   r.h.d.o.b.
   From its firm base as soon as I.
                        sus.

Large expansion generally prefers both hands, but may, under tranquil circumstances, sometimes be indicated with one hand. In moderate expansion, one hand is usually adequate.

Universality in unity may, for the most part, be expressed with one hand; universality in plurality generally requires both hands.

II. Unfolding, Displaying, etc.

Ex.—1. The landscape, OUTSTRETCHING IN LOVELINESS, lay on the lap of the year in the beauty of MAY.

2. His purposes will ripen *fast*,
      b. h. h. o.
   UNFOLDING EVERY HOUR.
      b. h. h. l.

3. One of the chief objects of interest was the magnificent DISPLAY OF NATIONAL BANNERS.

4. Look on this beautiful WORLD and read the *truth* in her fair
      b. h. h. l.   b. h. h. f.
   pages.
   sus.

5. All the proud virtue of this VAUNTING WORLD
      b. h. h. l.

   Fawns on success and power, *howe'er* acquired.
   b. h. d. o.   b. h. d. l.

Both Hands Ascending Front Supine.
(FIG. 28.)

I. Earnest Sacred Address — Appeal, Adoration, Ascription, Praise, Thanksgiving, Confession, Supplication, etc.

Ex.—1. We appeal to THEE, Thou righteous Judge.

2. Father Supreme, Thou ONLY God !

3. We render Thee praise and THANKSGIAING.

4. Against THEE, Thee ONLY have I sinned, and done this evil in Thy sight.

5. Lord, I have called DAILY upon Thee, I have STRETCHED OUT MY HANDS unto Thee.

6. HEAR my cry, and give EAR to the voice of my supplication.

7. Into THINE hand I commit my spirit.

FIG. 28.

The object here is to lay down the general principles of gesture, leaving the individual to determine for himself, according to his own feelings and sense of propriety, how much action to employ in addressing the Deity. The older divines were more demonstrative in this respect than those of the present day. Such gestures are more common in oblique than in direct discourse; as,

8. "O, HEAVEN!" he cried, "my bleeding COUNTRY save!"
   b. h. a. f.   rep.

II. Sacred Reference.

Ex.—1. In contemplation of *created* things, by steps we may ascend to
     GOD.   b. h. h. o.   slow prep.
     b. h. a. f.

2. Pay thy vows unto the MOST HIGH.

3. OF Him, and THROUGH Him, and TO Him are all things.
  b. h. a. f.   rep.   rep.   sus.

III. Elevation, Sacredness, Sublimity.

Ex.—1. Auspicious HOPE! in thy sweet garden grow
         b. h. a. f.

    WREATHS for each toil, a charm for every *woe*.
    rep.   b. h. d. o.

2. O, sacred TRUTH, thy triumphs *ceased* awhile.
   b. h. a. f.   b. h. d. f.

3. And hence, in middle heaven remote, is seen
    The mount of GOD, in awful glory BRIGHT.

Both Hands Ascending Oblique Supine.

(FIG. 29.)

FIG. 29.

General Elevation and Sublimity, Sublime Apostrophe, Devotional Address.

Ex.—1. Behold the everlasting HILLS.

2. The gathering clouds, like meeting ARMIES, come on apace.

3. Mutual *love*, the CROWN of all our
   b. h. h. o.　　　b. h. a. o.
   BLISS.

4. Legions of ANGELS shall guard you home.

5. HAIL, holy Light! offspring of HEAVEN, first-born.

6. Ye STARS, which are the poetry of HEAVEN.

7. The windows of HEAVEN were opened.

8. Open unto me the gates of RIGHTEOUSNESS.

9.　　　O LIBERTY,
   　　　b. h. a. o.
   Parent of happiness, CELESTIAL born ;
   　　　　　rep.
   When the first man became a living soul,
   His sacred GENIUS thou.
   　　　rep.

10. HAIL ! universal Lord !

Many of the uses assigned to the horizontal line of gesture, as fulness, abundance, comparison, etc., when combined with elevation or sublimity, would, of course, take the ascending instead of the horizontal.

Both Hands Ascending Lateral Supine.
(FIG. 30.)

I. Elevation, Sacredness, or Sublimity, combined with the Utmost Expansion, or with very large numbers or space.

Ex.—1. *Hail* to the joyous day! with
    b. h. a. o.
        purple clouds
    The WHOLE HORIZON glows.
        b. h. a. l.

2. Jehovah dwells in light and glory
    INEFFABLE.

3. O'er all those WIDE-EXTENDED
    PLAINS
    Shines one eternal DAY.

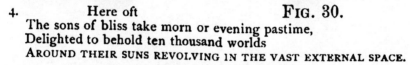

FIG. 30.

4.   Here oft
    The sons of bliss take morn or evening pastime,
    Delighted to behold ten thousand worlds
    AROUND THEIR SUNS REVOLVING IN THE VAST EXTERNAL SPACE.

5. *One* sun by day, by night TEN THOUSAND shine.
    r. h. a. f.   b. h. a. l.
6.   Heaven OPENED WIDE
    Her ever-during gates.

Here we have opening without external force, therefore the hands are supine. The emotion of joy may be added by quickening the movement.

II. Joy or Exultation in the highest degree. The boldest style of Triumph.

Ex.—1. JOY, joy FOREVER! my task is done—
    The gates are passed and HEAVEN is won!

2. Cherubic *legions* guard him home,
    b. h. a. o.
    And shout him WELCOME to the skies!
        b. h. a. l.

3. Through the vast of HEAVEN
    It sounded, and the faithful armies rung
    HOSANNA TO THE HIGHEST!

CHAPTER VI.

RIGHT HAND PRONE.

FIG. 31.

The primary signification of the prone hand is Superposition or Superincumbency. First, we have the physical representation of one thing placed or lying upon another, as in the following example:

The thunder clouds CLOSED O'ER IT.
b. h. h. o. prone.

Analogous to this is the intellectual or moral condition; as,

The cloud of adversity threw its gloom OVER ALL HIS PROSPECTS.
r. h. h. l. prone.

Tracing the analogy still farther, we come to the realm of feeling and emotion. While the supine hand expresses naked truth—the bare thought, or intellectual idea—the prone clothes the thought with some repressive emotion, as scorn, grief, sadness, or any sentiment of a grave, solemn or subdued character.

Compare the following examples:

> 1. I REJECT the imputation.
>   r. h. d. l. supine.
>
> 2. I reject the imputation with SCORN.
>   r. h. d. l. prone.

Compare also the following:

> 1. He was an eye WITNESS to that scene.
>   r. h. h. l. supine.
>
> 2. He was an eye WITNESS to that solemn scene.
>   r. h. h. l. prone.

Associations requiring the prone position of the hand may be expressed in words, or suggested by the context, or they may grow out of the speaker's feelings, or his knowledge of accompanying circumstances. The idea of superposition—physical or moral—may exist only by implication, as when the object referred to is supposed to be beneath some other object.

The relation of the prone to the supine hand may, in general terms, be thus stated:

The supine hand is communicative, and has the power of address; the prone is repressive.

The supine is permissory; the prone is prohibitory.

The supine is impulsive; the prone is compulsive.

The supine is genial; the prone is aversive.

The signification of the prone hand as compared with the supine is further illustrated by the following examples:

> 1. Speak FORTH.
>   r. h. h. f. supine.
>
> 2. Keep SILENCE.
>   r. h. h. f. prone.
>
> 3. 'T was MUSICAL, but SADLY sweet.
>   r. h. a. o. supine.   r. h. a. o. prone.

4. A talebearer REVEALETH secrets ; but he that is of a faithful
              r. h. h. o. supine.

    spirit CONCEALETH the matter.
         r. h. h. o. prone.

5. And it opened its fan-like leaves to THE LIGHT,
                         r. h. h. l. supine.

    And CLOSED them beneath the kisses of night.
        r. h. h. l. prone.   sus.

6. Now green in YOUTH, now withering on the GROUND.
          r. h. h. o. supine   r. h. d. o. prone.

7.   HUSH ! breathe it not ALOUD,
      h. f. prone.   h. o. prone.

    The wild WINDS must not hear it !   Yet AGAIN
          h. l. prone.   h. f. supine.

    I tell thee—we are FREE !
        b. h. h. l. supine.

Right Hand Descending Front Prone.

(FIG. 32.)

FIG. 32.

I. Suppression, Depression, Dejection, and kindred ideas.

Ex.—1. Put DOWN the unworthy feeling.

    2. Even Genius itself then feels rebuked and SUBDUED as in the presence of higher qualities.

II. Imprecation, Destruction.

Ex.—1. May curses BLAST thy arm,

    2. Thy money PERISH with thee !

    3. DUST thou art, and unto dust shalt thou RETURN.

    4. DOWN with the tyrant.

Right Hand Descending Oblique Prone.
(Fig. 33.)

I. Superposition, physical or moral.

Ex.—1. Yet on the ROSE's humble bed,
The sweetest dews of NIGHT are shed.

2. The storm of grief bears HARD upon his youth,
And BENDS him like a drooping flower to earth.

3. DEATH lies on her like an untimely
    d. o. p.
    FROST
     imp.
Upon the sweetest flower of all the field.

4. Like sheep they are laid in the GRAVE ;
DEATH shall feed on them.

5. These lofty *trees* wave not less *proudly*
     h. o.   h. l.
That their ancestors MOULDER BENEATH them.
                      d. o. p.

6. Truth crushed to EARTH shall *rise* again.
          d. o. p.   h. o.

7. Religion raises men *above* themselves; irreligion sinks them
beneath the BRUTES. a. o.
    d. o. p.

8. That power is used not to *benefit* mankind, but to CRUSH them.
    h. l. s.   d. o. p.

FIG. 33.

II. Prostration.

Ex.—1. Lo ! the *tyrant* prostrate on the DUST.
    d. o. ind.   d. o. p.

2. Like the dust before the *whirlwind* those men fly
                    a. l. s.
That prostrate on the ground of FORTUNE lie.
                    d. o. p.

III. Suppression, Repression, etc., generalized.

Ex.—1. Let every true patriot REPRESS such a feeling.

2. Their spirits were depressed by the weight of ADVERSITY.

3. The enemy was completely SUBDUED.

5*

4. Man on his brother's HEART hath trod.

5. Thou shalt tread upon the lion and ADDER; the young lion and the dragon shalt thou trample under FEET.

IV. General Imprecation, Utter Destruction, Destruction by Violence.

Ex.—1. Be *ready*, gods, with all your *thunder*-bolts,
 b. h. a. o.   rep.
 Dash him to PIECES !
 r. h. d. o. p.

2. BLASTED be such hopes !

3. They shall be punished with everlasting DESTRUCTION.

Right Hand Descending Lateral Prone.

(FIG. 34.)

FIG. 34.

I. Superposition.

Ex.—1. The hand of affection shall SMOOTH THE TURF for your last pillow.

2. Blessed is the man whose transgression is *forgiven*, whose sin is COVERED. d. l. s.

II. Cessation, Dissolution—Destruction without violence.

Ex.—1. The tumult CEASED !

2. GRADUAL SINKS THE BREEZE INTO A PERFECT CALM.

Slow movement of the hand outward and downward throughout the entire sentence.

3. FLED is the blasted verdure of the fields.

Here, as in the preceding example, the preparation precedes the voice ; but in this case the entire gesture is rapidly executed upon the first word.

4. I buried SORROW for his death in the GRAVE with him.

Reference to the grave may be made with any of the

descending gestures, the hand supine or prone, according to the associated idea or the degree of emotion.

5. Thus is my summer worn away and WASTED.

6.   How the *innocent*,
              h. o. s.
As in a gentle SLUMBER, pass away !
        d. l. p.

7. *At His rebuke* the billows DIE.
    r. h. and eyes uplifted.

8. Earth, that *nourished* thee, shall claim
          h. f.
Thy growth to be resolved to earth AGAIN.
             d. l. p.

III. Scorn, Contempt, Scornful Denial, or Rejection.

Ex.—1. I SCORN the base insinuation.

2. I reject the offer with DISDAIN.

3. I DESPISE an action so mean.

Right Hand Descending Oblique Backwards Prone.

(FIG. 35.)

Abhorrence, Detestation, Abhorrent Repression, Scornful and Contemptuous Rejection, etc.

Ex.—1. Thy threats I *scorn ;* thy mercies I
    DESPISE.   d. l. p.
    d. o. b. p.

2. Tell me I *hate* the bowl ;
        d. o.
Hate is a *feeble* word :
        d. l.
I *loathe*, ABHOR.
d. l. p. d. o. b. p.

3. DOWN, tempting fiend !

4. I reject the imputation with scorn and
    CONTEMPT.

FIG. 35.

In the third example the face and eyes are turned in the direction of the gesture ; in the other examples they are averted, as in fig. 35.

Right Hand Horizontal Front Prone.

(FIG. 36.)

FIG. 36.

I. Restraining, Arresting, Refraining, Seizing, Checking, Prohibiting, and the like; usually in connection with direct personal address. The accompanying figure shows this gesture in its mildest form, as adapted to unemphatic speech, as in the example "Step softly," etc. In more emphatic utterance, the hand and arm, and, it may be, the whole body, are projected forward with a degree of energy proportioned to the sentiment.

Ex.—1. RESTRAIN the unhallowed propensity.

2. ARREST the wandering thought.

3. REFRAIN, I entreat you, REFRAIN from such a course.

4. Seize the fleeting angel FAST, nor let him go.

5. CHECK the raging passion.

6. HUSH, boding voice!

7. PEACE! be STILL!

8. Step SOFTLY, that the blind mole hear not a FOOT-FALL.

9. Speak GENTLY!

10. Tread LIGHTLY, speak LOW, the old man is dying.

11. Be not RASH with thy mouth.

12. Teach NOT thy lips such scorn.

13. STAY thy impious hand!

14. STAND, Bayard! STAND!

15. O, *Hamlet*, speak NO MORE.
    h. f. s.   h. f. p.

16. I FORBID the alliance.

17. TOUCH not, TASTE not, HANDLE not.

II. Sacredness, Solemnity, Awe, or whatever tends to subdue the feelings.

Ex.—1. Take off thy SHOES from off thy feet : the place whereon thou standest is HOLY-ground.

2. Let the awe of the DIVINE HAND be upon you.

3. Down the dark FUTURE, through long GENERATIONS,
   The echoing sounds grow FAINTER, and then cease.
                                            drop.

4. O, BLINDNESS to the future ! *kindly* given
       h. f. p.   h. o. s.
   ·That each may *fill the circle marked by Heaven*.
       h. l. s.

III. Execration.

Ex.—1. The worm of conscience STILL BE-GNAW THY SOUL !

2. Proud city thou art DOOMED ! the curse of JOVE, a living, lasting CURSE is on thee !

IV. Deprecation.

Ex.—Let not thine ANGER burn against thy servant.

Right Hand Horizontal Oblique Prone.
(FIG. 37.)

I. Restraining, Arresting, etc., as in the preceding gesture, generalized.

Ex.—1. I charge you as men, and as Christians, to lay a RESTRAINT upon all such dispositions.

2.   Friendship has a power
   To SOOTHE AFFLICTION in her darkest hour.

II. Sacredness, Solemnity, Awe, Sadness, etc., generalized.

Ex.—1. How SOLEMN these scenes !

2. His terrors keep the world in AWE !

In this second example, the language is regarded as but a slight remove from didactic discourse : hence we employ

FIG. 37.

this mild form of gesture. The emotion of awe **may** demand quite a different style of action, as will be seen hereafter.

3. SPEECHLESS he stood, and PALE.

4. As a cloud *darkens the sky*, so sorrow casts a gloom over the SOUL.
a. o. p.   h. o. p.

Right Hand Horizontal Lateral Prone.

(FIG. 38.)

FIG. 38.

I. Extension in time, space or thought, combined with Superposition, Superincumbency, or with analogous mental or moral conditions; Descriptive Reference.

Ex.—1. The golden light of evening lay OVER THE WHOLE VALLEY.

2. The cloud of adversity threw its gloom OVER ALL HIS PROSPECTS.

3. From the center to the far off horizon of his POWER he could see nothing but the DESOLATIONS he had made.

4. Now fades the glimmering LANDSCAPE on the sight.

5. The silent heart which *grief* assails,
h. o. p.

Treads SOFT AND LONESOME O'ER THE VALE.
h. l. p.

II. Distant Reference combined with Superposition, or with Repression, Gloom, Dejection, etc.

In referring to a distant locality, the straight line is sometimes more effective than the curve, for the executionary movement. In extension, the curve is necessary in order to indicate the intervening space. The line from the head to the hand, in fig. 38, may, therefore, curve or not, according to circumstances.

Ex.—1. Something of SADNESS wrapped the spot.

    2. When far from the parental roof, the youth paused and REFLECTED upon his course.

    3. Mercy WEPT over the melancholy scene!

    4. What pale DISTRESS afflicts those wretched isles!
          h. l. p.
    There hope ne'er DAWNS, and pleasure never SMILES.

    5. With eyes upraised, as one inspired,
    Pale Melancholy sat RETIRED.

III. Removal, Withdrawal, etc.

Ex.—1. Put AWAY from thee a froward mouth.

    2. When the *wicked* rise, men HIDE themselves.
       h. o.   h. l. p.

    3. The sun WITHDREW his cheering ray.

Right Hand Horizontal Oblique Backwards Prone.
(FIG. 39.)

This gesture is employed much the same as the preceding one, except that it expresses ideas requiring a wider sweep of the hand. Its special signification is Remoteness in time or space, combined with Superposition, or with any repressive emotions.

Ex.—The wickedness of the ANTEDILUVIAN
          h. o. b. p.
    world provoked the judgments of
Heaven.
 a. f. p.

FIG. 39.

Right Hand Ascending Front Prone.
(FIG. 40.)

Supernal Restraint, or Prohibition.

Ex.—Justice cries FORBEAR!

FIG. 40.   FIG. 41.   FIG. 42.

Right Hand Ascending Oblique Prone.
(FIG. 41.)

I. Elevation, combined with Superposition, or Repression, or analogous ideas.

Ex.—1. The rising moon has HID THE STARS.

    2. And THOU, pale moon! turn PALER at the sound.
      r. h. a. o.   r. h. a. o. p.

II. Supernal Restraint, or Prohibition generalized.

Ex.—Ye gods, WITHHOLD your wrath!

Right Hand Ascending Lateral Prone.
(FIG. 42.)

Elevation or Sublimity combined with Distance or Extension, and associated with Superposition or Repression.

Ex.—1. The mountain top was wrapped in MISTS.

2. So darkly glooms yon *thunder* cloud,

a. l. ind.

That SWATHES AS WITH A PURPLE SHROUD,

a. l. p.

Benledi's distant *hill.*

a. l. ind.

3. I had a dream that was not *all* a dream;

raise and drop the hand.

The bright sun was *extinguished,* and the stars

d. o. p.

Did wander, darkling in the ETERNAL SPACE

a. l. p.

Rayless and *pathless,* and the icy earth

drop.

Swung blind and BLACKENING in the moonless air.

a. l. p.

Right Hand Ascending Oblique Backwards Prone.
(FIG. 43.)

Remoteness in time or space combined with Elevation or Sublimity, and associated with Superposition, or with any repressive emotion.

Ex.—1. Wrapped in the mists of the remotest ANTIQUITY.

2. On my flight, through utter and through middle DARKNESS borne.

3. The law was given amidst the thunderings of SINAI.

FIG. 43.

CHAPTER VII.

BOTH HANDS PRONE.

Both Hands Descending Front Prone.
(FIG. 44.)

Superposition, Suppression, etc.

EXAMPLES.—1. (*Gentle Emotion.*) GREEN be the turf above thee.
2. Lie LIGHTLY on her, Earth—her step was light on thee.
3. (*Vehement Emotion.*) BURIED be the unworthy thought for ever !

FIG. 44.   FIG. 45.

Both Hands Descending Oblique Prone.
(FIG. 45.)

I. Superposition, Suppression. Embracing larger numbers or more space than the gesture in front.

Ex.—1. BURIED be all such thoughts.

    2. To *prevail* in the cause that is dearer than life,
        b. h. h. o.

    Or be crush'd in its RUINS to DIE !
        b. h. d. o. p.

II. Prostration.

Ex.—1.   They forthwith to the place
    Repairing where he judged them, PROSTRATE fell
    Before him REVERENT.
        imp.

    2. Sons of *dust*, in REVERENCE bow !
        b. h. h. o.   b. h. d. o. p.

Both Hands Descending Lateral Prone.
(FIG. 46.)

I. Superposition or Superincumbency, physical or moral.

Ex.—1. Thou hast forgiven the iniquity of Thy people ; Thou hast COVERED all their sin.

    2. If we attempt to compass the idea of *eternity*, we are OVER-
        b. h. a. l.   b. h. d. l. p.
    WHELMED by the contemplation of a theme so vast.

FIG. 46.

    3.   The golden *sun*,
        a. f.
    The *planets*, all the infinite host
    a. o.
    of *heaven*,
    b. h. a. l.
    Are shining on the sad abodes of
    DEATH.
    b. h. d. l. p.

II. Privation, Deprivation, Divesting, and the like, when accompanied with strong emotion, prefer the prone to the supine, and express themselves with this style of gesture.

Ex.—1. Alas ! how poor and little worth, .
    b. h. upl.
    Are all these glittering toys of EARTH.

    2. O may I no longer dreaming,
      Idly WASTE my golden days !

To describe, here, the slow process of wasting, there should be a softening or smoothing of the gesture— a slow motion of the hands.

III. Cessation, Dissolution, Utter Destruction, etc.

Ex.—1. Here let the tumults of passion forever CEASE !
    2. This great fabric shall be DISSOLVED !
    3. He uttered *his* voice, the earth MELTED.
      a. f.
    4. Death levels ALL THINGS in his march.
    5. All things decay with TIME.

IV. Extreme Humility, Self-abasement.

Ex.—Wherefor I ABHOR myself, and repent in dust and ASHES.

V. Renunciation, Hopeless Relinquishment, Utter Abandonment, Despair.

Ex.—1. I utterly renounce all HOPE.
    2. Without shedding of blood there is no REMISSION.

Both Hands Horizontal Front Prone.
(FIG. 47.)

I. Superposition, etc.

Ex.—On horror's head horrors ACCUMULATE.

II. Benediction (upon an individual).

Ex.—A father's choicest BLESSINGS rest on thee.

III. Execration.

Ex.—Take with thee thy most heavy CURSE,
    Which in the day of battle tire thee more
    Than all the complete ARMOUR that thou wear'st !

IV. Deprecation.

Ex.—PAUSE ! I implore you, PAUSE !

FIG. 47.

Both Hands Horizontal Oblique Prone.
(FIG. 48.)

I. Superposition.

Ex.—The veil of night CAME SLOWLY DOWN.

II. Benediction.

Ex.—Heaven's choicest BLESSINGS rest upon you all.

III. Execration.

Ex.—Heaven's heaviest CURSE shall fall on you.

FIG. 48.   FIG. 49.

Both Hands Horizontal Lateral Prone.
(FIG. 49.)

Extension combined with Superposition; hence, Diffusion, Desolation.

Ex.—1. O'er all the peaceful WORLD the smile of heaven shall lie.

2. Spread WIDE AROUND the heaven breathing calm.

3. Gold SOWED THE WORLD WITH EVERY ILL.

4.   Horror WIDE EXTENDS
His desolate domain.

Both Hands Ascending Front Prone.
(FIG. 50.)

I. Sacred Ascription, or Attribution.

Ex.—Thou art clothed with LIGHT as with a garment.

II. Sacred Deprecation.

Ex.—WITHHOLD thy merited wrath.

FIG 50.   FIG. 51.

Both Hands Ascending Oblique Prone.
(FIG. 51.)

I. Superposition, etc.

Ex.—1. Hung be the heavens with BLACK.

    2. *Save* me and HOVER OVER ME WITH YOUR WINGS,
    b. h. a. o.   b. h. a. o. p.
    Ye heavenly guards !

II. Sacred Ascription.

Ex.—Glory and HONOR and might and dominion and POWER be unto
    Him that sitteth upon the throne.

III. Sacred or Sublime Deprecation.

Ex.—Ye gods, RESTRAIN your wrath.

Both Hands Ascending Lateral Prone.
(FIG. 52.)

Elevation or Sublimity, and Extension or Expansion, combined with Superposition.

Ex.—1. And let the triple rainbow rest O'ER ALL THE MOUNTAIN TOPS.

2. The floor of Heaven BE-STREWN WITH GOLDEN STARS.

FIG. 52.

CHAPTER VIII.

THE VERTICAL HAND.

FIG. 53.

While the prone hand puts down, the vertical drives away. The former makes the repressive gesture, the latter the repellant. Owing to the impracticability of using the vertical hand in the descending lines, such gestures are excluded from this system. We therefore commence with the horizontal.

Right Hand Horizontal Front Vertical.
(FIG. 54.)

Repulsion.

EXAMPLE.—Back to thy PUNISHMENT, false fugitive !

Right Hand Horizontal Oblique Vertical.

(FIG. 55.)

Aversion, General Repulsion.

Ex.— 1. He generously extended the arm of power to ward OFF the blow.

2. Drive BACK the bold invaders !

3. The face of the Lord is AGAINST them that do evil.

4. Murder most *foul*, as in the *best* it is ;
   r. h. d. o. p.   r. h. d. o. s.

But this MOST FOUL, strange and *unnatural*.
   r. h. h. o. v.   r. h. d. o. p.

FIG. 54.   FIG. 55.   FIG. 56.

Right Hand Horizontal Lateral Vertical.

(FIG. 56.)

Removal, Repulsion, Aversion.

In intense aversion the face should be turned away from the object.

Ex.—1. Thou tempting fiend, AVAUNT !

2. I REPEL the base insinuation.

6

3. I hate and ABHOR lying, but Thy law do I *love*.
   h. l. v.   b. h. h. f. s.

4. HENCE, Jealousy ; thou fatal lying fiend,
   Thou false seducer of our hearts, BEGONE !

5. O, that way MADNESS lies ; let me SHUN that ;
   no MORE of that.

While the notation of this last example indicates a repetition of the gesture upon certain words, it should be observed that language of this kind admits of a succession of nervous repetitions, without reference to the emphatic words. Impatience frequently manifests itself in this manner.

Right Hand Horizontal Oblique Backwards Vertical.

(FIG. 57.)

FIG. 57.

I. Removal, Retrogression, etc. Usually associated with Remoteness.

Ex.—1. We BANISH you our territories.

2. When driven by *oppression's* rod,
   h. l. v.
   Our fathers FLED BEYOND THE SEA.
   h. o. b. v.

II. Repulsion, specially Abhorrent Repulsion.

Ex.—1. When mine enemies are turned BACK,
   h. o. b. v.
   they shall fall and *perish* at thy presence.
   d. o. b. p.

2. Get thee BEHIND me, Satan !

Right Hand Ascending Front Vertical.

(FIG. 58.)

Sacred Deprecation.

Ex.—AVERT Thy sore displeasure.

Right Hand Ascending Oblique Vertical.

(FIG. 59.)

Sacred or Sublime Deprecation.

Ex.—FORBID it, Heaven.

It will be observed that this language is impersonal; hence it prefers the oblique to the front.

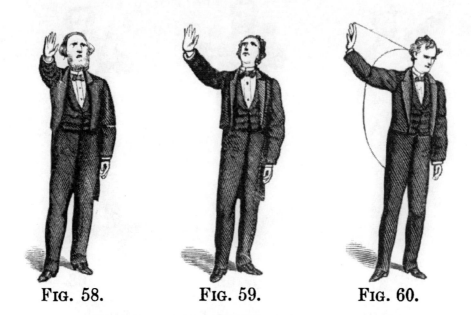

FIG. 58. FIG. 59. FIG. 60.

Right Hand Ascending Lateral Vertical.

(FIG. 60.)

Aversion, Repulsion, or Removal, etc., combined with Elevation.

Ex.—1. AWAY, delusive phantom!

2. Fly HENCE, ye idle brood of folly!

3. The strong arm of the mighty Conqueror REPELLED the Prince of the Power of the air.

4. The silent hour steals on,
   slow prep.
   And flaky darkness BREAKS WITHIN THE EAST.

Right Hand Ascending Oblique Backwards Vertical.
(FIG. 61.)

Repulsion and Elevation, Abhorrent Repulsion.

Ex.—HENCE, horrible shadow!
    Unreal mockery, HENCE!

FIG. 61.   FIG. 62.   FIG. 63.

Both Hands Horizontal Front Vertical.
(FIGS. 62, 63.)

I. Forcible Repulsion.

Ex.—1. The torrent *roar'd*, and we did BUFFET it
         b. h. h. o. s.   b. h. h. f. v.
    With LUSTY sinews; throwing it *aside*,
         rep.   b. h. h. o. v.
    And STEMMING it with hearts of controversy.
    b. h. h. f. v.
  2. Thou impious mocker, HENCE!

II. This gesture, in common with the corresponding
oblique (b. h. h. o. v.) is the natural expression of Fear
and Terror. The hands are first drawn near to the face,

and then thrust forcibly towards the object, while the body starts back.   See fig. 63.

Ex.—Whence and what art thou, execrable shape !

Both Hands Horizontal Oblique Vertical.
(Fig. 64.)

General Repulsion, Fear, etc.

Ex.—1. Far from our hearts be so inhuman a feeling.

2. Repel the base invaders.

FIG. 64.

FIG. 65.

FIG. 66.

Both Hands Horizontal Lateral Vertical.
(FIG. 66.)

Expansion, Disruption, Dispersion.

In emphatic or impassioned discourse the hands, in preparation for this gesture, may sometimes cross the breast, as in fig. 65.   In general, however, the ordinary preparation will suffice.   When the hands cross the body, as shown in the cut, they should not be allowed to rest in this position, but should pass and repass each other more or less rapidly, according to the force and rapidity of the accompanying utterance.

Ex.—1. The gate of Death in SUNDER breaks !

2.   And if the night
   Have gathered aught of evil or concealed,
   DISPERSE it, as now light dispels the DARK.

Both Hands Ascending Front Vertical.
(FIG. 67.)

Earnest Sacred Deprecation.

Ex.—AVERT, O God, the frown of Thine indignation.

FIG. 67.   FIG. 68.

Both Hands Ascending Oblique Vertical.
(FIG. 68.)

I. Deprecation combined with Elevation or Sublimity.

Ex.—Let me not NAME it to you, ye chaste stars.

II. Fear, Terror, etc.

Ex.—1. How DREADFUL is this place!

    2. Angels and ministers of grace, DEFEND US!

    3.   Alarmed, AFRAID,
    I see the flashes of Thy LIGHTNING wild!

Both Hands Ascending Lateral Vertical.
(FIG. 69.)

Elevation and Expansion combined, Dispersion, Disruption.

The hands, in preparation for this gesture, sometimes cross the body as in fig. 65.

Ex.—1. The mists of morning are DISPERSED by the rising sun.

    2. Melt and DISPEL, ye spectre doubts.

    3. BURSTS the wild cry of terror and dismay!

FIG. 69.

CHAPTER IX.

SPECIAL GESTURES.

In addition to the systematic gestures described in the preceding chapters, we have what may be called Special Gestures. These are so numerous as to preclude an exhaustive enumeration. The following are the most important :

Right Hand Uplifted Vertical.
(FIG. 70.)

FIG. 70.

The vertical hand is here presented with the palm nearly facing the left of the speaker, instead of being outward as those in Chapter VIII. The position of the hand and arm at the terminus of this gesture is similar to the ordinary preparation (compare figs. 6 and 70). By virtue of its peculiar signification, however, this constitutes a distinct gesture. It should be specially observed that here the hand is brought *up* to the terminal point without any preparatory action, while in the systematic gestures, and some others, it is brought *down* to the point indicated in the notation, having been previously raised higher in preparation. The hand is raised with the palm downward, until it nearly reaches the destined point, when there is an additional turn of the wrist-joint, which finishes the gesture by throwing the hand into the vertical position. The freedom of the wrist in the execution of this last movement gives additional effect.

Fig. 70 shows the uplifted hand as brought up on the front line to the position ascending front. It may take the front or oblique, according to the sentiment. The front implies more elevation, and the oblique more expansion. Sacredness and solemnity generally prefer the front, sublimity the oblique. In moderate expression the hand may be arrested at the horizontal line, thus giving four gestures under this head; ascending front, ascending oblique, horizontal front, horizontal oblique.

The uplifted hand has the following significations:

I. Adjuration, Oath, Solemn Declaration.

EXAMPLES.—1. I ADJURE THEE, BY THE LIVING GOD, that thou come
r. h. upl. a. f. v.
out of her.
r. h. d. f. s.

2. I SWEAR I will not see it *lost !*
r. h. upl. a. f. v.   d. f.

3. I have SWORN AN OATH, that I will have my *bond.*
r. h. upl. a. f. v.   r. h. d. f. cli.

4. BY ALL MY HOPES, most falsely doth he *lie !*
r. h. upl. a. f. v.   r. h. d. f. cli.

5. *Rouse,* ye Romans ! rouse, ye *slaves !*   Once again I
b. h. h. o.   b. h. d. o.
SWEAR the Eternal City *shall* be free.
r. h. upl. a. f. v.   d. f.

6*

6. BLESSED is the man whose transgression is *forgiven.*
r. h. upl. a. o. v.   d. o.

II. The uplifted hand serves to Arrest Attention, as in the exclamations, Hark! See! and the like. It also accompanies an Arousing Call or Command, and is used in Exclamations generally.

Ex.—1. HARK to the joyous strain!

2. HO.! sound the *tocsin* from the tower.
r. h. upl. a. o. v.   r. h. a. o. ind.

3. QUICK! man the *life-boat!*
r. h. upl. a. o. v.   r. h. h. o. ind.

4. HOW MISERABLE is man when the foot of the *conqueror* is on his
r. h. upl. a. o. v.   d. o. ind.
neck,
What black DESPAIR, what HORROR fills his heart!
r. h. upl. h. o. v.   r. h. upl. a. o. v.

In arresting attention, when the emotion is sudden and vivid, the index finger may take the place of the open hand. In this case the hand is suddenly raised, the finger pointing to the hearer, the eye at the same instant turning in the direction of the sound.

Ex.—HARK! heard ye not that piercing cry?

III. Arrested Preparation. The uplifted hand may, either by accident or design, become the preparation for a gesture.

Ex.—1. HOW GREAT THE LOVE that Him inclined to bleed and *die* for me!
r. h. upl. a. o.   d. o.
2. As I LIVE, saith the Lord, I have no *pleasure* in the death of the
r. h. upl. a. f.   d. f.
wicked.

In these examples the hand is raised in exclamation and in solemn affirmation, the sustained gesture serving, incidentally, as an arrested preparation, until the hand is brought down upon the emphatic word. See also the examples under Adjuration, etc.

Both Hands Uplifted Vertical.

(FIG. 71.)

This also takes the front and the oblique, ascending or horizontal according to the sentiment. Fig. 71 exhibits the ascending oblique; the palms nearly face each other.

I. Serious, Earnest, Sublime and Sacred Aspirations; Awe, Wonder, Surprise, Admiration, Pity, Horror, etc., when moderate, employ this style of gesture in the horizontal line; when extreme, they use the ascending. Profound Reverence, Adoration, Blessing, and other forms of sacred or solemn address, also employ the uplifted hands.

FIG. 71.

Ex.—1. O THAT THIS LOVELY VALE WERE MINE!
  b. h. upl. h. o. v.

 2. HOW BEAUTIFUL is all this visible world!
  b. h. upl. h. o. v.

 3. IN WINTER AWFUL THOU!
  b. h. upl. a. o. v.

 4. GREAT GOD, how infinite Thou art!
  b. h. upl. a. f. v.

 5. GREAT AND MARVELOUS are Thy works.
  b. h. upl. a. o. v.

In profound reverence and awe the hands are raised very slowly, and for a considerable time held motionless; the eyes, at the same time, are upraised, the whole posture harmonizing with the general character of the discourse.

 6. O HOW BEAUTIFUL is this midnight scene!
  b. h. upl. a. o. v.

7.   SCENE SUBLIME !
       b. h. upl. a. o. v.
Where the rich earth presents her golden *treasure*.
                   b. h. h. o. s.

8. THE FLOODS have lifted up their voice.
     b. h. upl. a. o. v.

9. O, HORRIBLE ! horrible ! most horrible !
     b. h. upl. a. o. v.

10. HOLY, HOLY, HOLY, LORD GOD OF SABAOTH !

11. BLESSED BE THY NAME, O Lord most high.
     b. h. upl. a. f. v.

12. BLESSED are all they that put their trust in *Him*.
   b. h. upl. a. o. v.   b. h. a. f. s.

13.   HEAVEN AND EARTH will witness,
       b. h. upl. a. o. v.

If Rome *must* fall, we are *innocent.*
   b. h. h. o.   b. h. d. o.

It will be observed that the same notation is given for sentiments entirely different from each other, as surprise and pity, admiration and horror. These apparent incongruities will be adjusted by the various modes of execution, as quick or slow, and the accompanying variations in voice, attitude and facial expression.

II. Benediction, especially when brief. The horizontal elevation is sufficient.

Ex.—HEAVEN GRANT YOU SUCCESS.

In more full and solemn benediction, the regular gesture, b. h. h. o. p., or the uplifted prone, is preferable.

III. An Arousing Call or Summons is accompanied by an upward sweep of the hands, corresponding with the present gesture.

Ex.—RISE ! or Greece for ever *falls !*
   b. h. upl.   b. h. d. o.
UP ! or freedom breathes her *last !*
   b. h. upl.   b. h. d. o.

Both Hands Uplifted Vertical, Palms Outward.

(FIG. 72.)

Here also the hands are elevated more or less, according to the degree of emotion. Fig. 72 shows the gesture in its most expressive form. Fig. 64 will serve to illustrate the same gesture in the horizontal elevation, supposing the hands to be thus raised without any preparatory movement. In common with the uplifted vertical, this is the natural language of Surprise, and usually takes precedence when surprise deepens into astonishment. Also employed in exclamations of Rapture.

FIG. 72.

Ex.—1. "LAND ! LAND !" cry the sailors.

2. With sudden START the miser wakes.

3. Then ope's his *chest*, with treasure stored,
   b. h. d. f.

   And stands in RAPTURE o'er his hoard.
   b. h. upl. a. o. v. out.

The corresponding gesture with one hand is often used to express a moderate degree of surprise or fear. See right hand in fig. 80.

Both Hands Uplifted Supine.

(FIG. 73.)

FIG. 73.

I. This is employed to describe the act of lifting up; being opposite in effect to putting down with the prone hand.

Ex.—With the lever of prayer resting on the fulcrum of faith, we can move the *world*, and LIFT IT
b. h. h. l.   b. h. upl. s.
UP TO GOD.

II. Admiration, when it arises from some extraordinary or unexpected circumstance, expresses itself in this manner. The hands are then thrown up suddenly, the face and eyes being upraised at the same time.

Ex.—   Rapturous sight !
Fresh *bursts* the New World from the darkness of night !
b. h. h. o.
O VISIONS OF GLORY ! how dazzling it seems !
b. h. upl. s.

Right Hand Uplifted Prone.

The hand is raised with the palm downward, retaining the prone position throughout, the arm, wrist and hand being moved as one. The degree of elevation varies with the sentiment.

Wonder, Surprise, Pity, etc., in a moderate degree, are sometimes expressed in this manner; the action being less than in the vertical, since it lacks the additional wrist movement. Regret is indicated by feebly raising and dropping the hand.

Ex.—1. ALAS! poor YORICK!
raise.   drop.

2. AH ELOQUENCE! thou wast UNDONE.
raise.   drop.

Both Hands Uplifted Prone.

This may follow either the front or the oblique line, and be elevated to the horizontal or to the ascending plane.

I. Appropriate in Benediction and other forms of Solemn Discourse. When the hands are raised slowly, the effect is more solemn than in the regular prone gesture as applied to benediction, etc.

Ex.—[Apostolic benediction.]

II. The feeble raising and dropping of both hands sometimes occurs in the expression of grief.

Ex.—FAREWELL! a long FAREWELL to all my greatness.
raise.   drop.

Both Hands Supine Parallel.
(FIGS. 74, 75, 76.)

FIG. 74.   FIG. 75.   FIG. 76.

This may be made in any of the following directions:
Descending oblique, to the right or left.   (Fig. 74.)
Descending lateral,   "   "   "
Horizontal oblique,   "   "   "
Horizontal lateral,   "   "   "   (Fig. 75.)
Ascending oblique,   "   "   "   (FIG. 76.)
Ascending lateral,   "   "   "

These are sometimes employed in impassioned reference, or any reference to the right or left of the speaker, where one hand is inadequate to the full expression, and needs to be supplemented by the other hand.

Ex.—1. Take her up TENDERLY,
   b. h. d. o. s. par.
  Lift her with CARE.
   b. h. h. o. s. par.

 2. THERE LIES HE ! go and LOOK !
  b. h. d. l. s. par.   rep.

 3. DEATH'S CHAIN is on your champion.
  b. h. d. l. s. par.

 4. THESE ARE THE HOMES of peaceful industry.
  b. h. h. l. s. par.

 5. Higher, HIGHER let us climb up the steep of knowledge.
  b. h. a. o. par.

 6. I dare him to his PROOFS !
  b. h. h. o. par.

 7. Cannon to RIGHT of them,
  b. h. h. l. par. (right)
  Cannon to LEFT of them.
  b. h. h. l. par. (left)

This style of gesture is also admissible in the direction oblique backwards.

Ex.—Cannon BEHIND them.

The supine hands accompanied with an attitude of courage and manliness, is preferable to the vertical hands, which some would employ, in order to express the emotion of terror at beholding this dreadful charge. The orator should possess himself of the courage of

" the noble six hundred," rather than to act the part of a terrified witness of the scene.

Both Hands Prone Parallel.
(Fig. 77.)

In these the arms assume the same relative positions, and move in the same directions, as in the parallel supine just described; the only difference being in the position of the hands. Fig. 77 represents the horizontal oblique. They are similar in application, with the additional power of expressing superposition and repressive emotions.

Ex.—The Lord hath laid on HIM the iniquity of us all.   b. h. h. o. p. par.

FIG. 77.

Both Hands Vertical Parallel.
(Figs. 78, 79.)

FIG. 78.   FIG. 79.

These correspond with the preceding, except the position of the hands, and their being limited to the horizontal and the ascending lines. Employed in Forcible Repulsion, in circumstances where both hands are required at either side of the speaker. Fig. 78 shows this gesture in the horizontal oblique, and 79 in the horizontal lateral.

Ex.—HENCE, hideous spectre.
    b. h. h. o. v. par.

The student may apply this style of action to many of the examples given under the regular vertical gestures, selecting the more impassioned sentences.

These three forms of parallel gestures—supine, prone and vertical—are analogous to what Austin terms principal and subordinate gestures; though they differ essentially from them in that both hands are here kept on the same plane, whereas Austin would have the principal gesture elevated one position higher than the subordinate, as when the left hand is in the direction descending oblique, and the right in the horizontal lateral. While no objection is here made to the style of action just mentioned, so far as the subordinate gesture is entirely involuntary—a faint echo, as it were, of the principal—as, for instance, in fig. 80, such gestures are purposely omitted from this treatise. Although admissible in some cases, they need not be made prominent in a system of rhetorical action.

FIG. 80.

Index Finger.
(FIGS. 81, 82, 83.)

FIG. 81.

FIG. 82.   FIG. 83.

I. The index finger, pointing in any direction suited to the occasion, is employed in Indication, from which it receives its name, in Special Designation, Specific Reference, Close Discrimination, Precision, Emphatic Designation, etc., serving not only to point out particular persons and objects, but, analogically, to call attention to particular ideas. The open hand in its outward sweep, is used to extend the thought; the index finger, to limit it. Compare the notation of the two following sentences:

   1. Let us survey the ENTIRE FIELD.
              r. h. h. l. s.

   2. Let us closely observe THIS point.
             h. f. ind.

The following miscellaneous examples will illustrate

the use of the index finger, according to the applications given above:

1. The full-orbed moon has reached no higher
   Than yon old CHURCH'S mossy spire.
   h. o. ind.

2. Mark yonder pomp of costly FASHION.
   h. l. ind.

3. In yonder GRAVE a Druid lies.
   h. l. ind.   sus.

4. Her fancy followed him *through foaming waves,*
   To distant SHORES.   h. l. s.
   h. l. ind.

5. *Hush!* HARK to that sound stealing faint through the wood.
   h. o. p.   h. l. ind.

Hush is always authoritative, and employs the repressive gesture; *hark* is the call for attention, and is merely earnest.

6. But LOOK, the morn in russet mantle clad,
   a. f. ind.
   Walks o'er the dew of yonder eastern HILL.
   rep.

7. See yon rising SUN.
   h. f. ind.

8. See yon setting SUN.
   h. o. b. ind.

9. See on yon darkening HEIGHTS bold Franklin tread.
   a. l. ind.

10. The puissant Michael vanquished APOLLYON upon the summit of
    the everlasting HILLS.   a. o. b. ind.
    imp.

11. He led the tyrant DEATH in chains.
    d. o. ind.

12. He PIERCES through the realms of light.
    a. o. ind.

13. Flashes of LIGHTNING played around the distant horizon. (Fig.83.)
    h. l. ind.

14. Sin may *gratify,* but repentance STINGS.
    h. o. s.   h. o. ind.

15. The keen eye of the statesman penetrated the FUTURE.
    h. f. ind.

16. For proof of my assertion, I point you back to days of the
    PROPHETS.
    h. o. b. ind.

17. I 've touched the HIGHEST point of all my greatness.
   a. f. ind.

18. A spirit of evil flashing DOWN,
   d. l. ind.
   With the lurid light of a fiery crown.

19. A mere air-drawn dagger of the FANCY.
   a. l. ind.

20. HOPE, like the glim'ring taper's light,
   a. f. ind.
   Adorns and *cheers* the way.
   a. o. s.

21. So Faith and Hope the self-same OBJECTS spy.
   a. f. ind.

22.   *Beyond* is all abyss,
   a. f. p.
   ETERNITY, whose end no eye can reach.
   a. f. ind.

23. And Nathan said·to David, THOU art the man.
   h. f. ind.

24. CLARENCE has come ! FALSE ! FLEETING ! PERJURED Clarence !
   h. f. ind.   rep.   rep.   rep.

25.   O that men's ears should be
   To COUNSEL deaf, but not to FLATTERY.
   h. o. ind.   h. l. ind.

26. See, how he sets his countenance for DECEIT.
   h. o. ind.
   And promises a lie before he SPEAKS.
   rep.

27.   Guards, *seize*
   h. f. p.
   This traitor, and convey him to the TOWER,
   h. l. ind.
   There let him learn OBEDIENCE.
   rep.

28. Read thy doom in the FLOWERS which fade and die.
   d. o. ind.

29. O, cursed lust of *gold!* when for thy sake
   b h. d. o.
   The wretch throws up his interest in *both* worlds;
   b. h. d. l.
   First HANGED in this, then DAMN'D in that to come.
   h. o. ind.   d. o. ind.

30. There 's the MARBLE, there 's the CHISEL;
   h. o. ind.   d. o. ind.
   Take them, work them at thy *will;*
   h. f. s.   rep.

Thou ALONE must shape thy future,—
h. f. ind.

Heaven give thee strength and *skill.*
r. h. upl.　　　　　　　　　　d. o. s.

31. He dares not touch a HAIR of Cataline.
h. o. ind.

32. Mark the PERFECT man.
h. o. ind.

33. THIS is the point to which I call your special ATTENTION.
h. f. ind.　　　　　　　　　　　　rep.

34. If this measure be *adopted* — MARK my word — our country will
be *ruined.*　　　h. f. s.　　h. f. ind.
d. f. s.

35. We have *promised*, but RECOLLECT, under certain RESTRICTIONS.
d. o. s.　　　　h. o. ind.　　　　　rep.

36. Let the thought be deeply engraved upon your HEART, that
h. f. ind.

every MOMENT which flies, is irrecoverably LOST.
rep.　　　　　　　　　　rep.

II. The index finger is used in Reproach, Scorn, Contempt, Derision, etc. The hand is then inverted, as in fig. 82. In earnest and serious discoure, it is sidewise, as in fig. 81.

Ex.—1. Thou SLAVE!
h. f. ind.

2. Yon trembling COWARD, who forsook his master.
h. o. b. ind.

3. There were FALSE prophets among the people.
h. l. ind.

4. VIPERS! that creep where man *disdains* to climb.
d. l. ind.　　　　　　　　　d. l. p.

5. Behold the TRAITOR!
h. o. ind.

6. Thou crawling WORM!
d. o. ind.

7.　　　　*One* murder makes a VILLAIN,
h. f. ind.　　　　　　h. l. ind.
Millions a *hero.*
b. h. h. o.　a. o. s.

8. Some sky-ward flight of SUPERSTITION.
a. l. ind.

9. The perpetrator of so base an act merits only the finger of
SCORN.
h. l. ind.

III. Cautioning, Warning, Threatening, Authoritative Prohibition or Prohibitory Warning.

The index finger thus employed is more forcible and defiant than the open hand.

In warning and threatening there may be an accompanying tremor of the finger.

Ex.—1. Timely *advised*, the coming evil SHUN.
　　　　h. o. s.　　　　　　　　h. o. ind.

2. Let every man take heed HOW he buildeth thereupon.
　　　　　　　　　　h. o. ind.

3. Lay not that FLATTERING unction to your soul.
　　　　　　h. f. ind.

4. BITTERLY shall you rue your folly.
　　h. f. ind.

5. 　　　　If thou speakest FALSE,
　　　　　　　　h. f. ind.

Upon the next TREE shalt thou hang ALIVE,
　　　　h. o. ind.　　　　　　　　rep.

Till FAMINE cling thee.
　　rep.

6. Lay not your hand upon the CONSTITUTION.
　　　　　　　　　h. f. ind.

In mild expression generally, and in emphatic discourse sometimes, prohibition prefers the prone hand.

7. LOCHIEL! Lochiel! BEWARE of the day
　h. f. ind.　　　　　rep.

When the LOWLANDS shall meet thee in battle array!
　　　　rep.

8. Take fast hold of INSTRUCTION; let her not GO; KEEP her, for
　　　　　　h. f. ind.　　　　　rep.　　rep.

she is thy LIFE.
　d. f. ind.

NOTE.—The gesture upon *life* is made in the descending line for special emphasis, and for consummation. To regard it as a gesture of designation in the sense of suggesting locality, would, of course, render the action entirely inappropriate. Unjust criticism based upon such misinterpretation, however, is likely to grow out of a superficial knowledge of the subject.

9. Look not thou upon the WINE when it is RED, when it giveth his
　　　　　　h. f. ind.　　　　　rep.

COLOR in the cup, when it MOVETH itself aright. At the last
　rep.　　　　　　　　h. o. s.

it biteth like a SERPENT and stingeth like an ADDER.
　　　d. o. ind.　　　　　　　　d. l. ind.

IV. Special Emphasis, Emphatic Assertion or Emphatic Distinction.

When thus used with energy the index finger is more emphatic than the open hand. In emphatic assertion it is generally confined to the descending lines, but when it serves the double purpose of special designation and special emphasis—emphatic designation—it may, as before stated, take any direction.

Examples of Special Emphasis:

1. I repeat it, sir, I will NEVER submit.
    d. f. ind.
2. The *truth* of this whole statement I do most emphatically DENY.
    h. f. ind.   d. f. ind.
3. The tyrannous and bloody act is DONE.
    d. f. ind.

In this use of the index finger the gesture must be *forcibly* executed, or the effect will be different from what is here intended: there will be danger of nullifying the action by running the gesture into one of designation, when there is no special object pointed out.

Right Hand Uplifted, Fore-Arm Vertical, and Index Finger Pointing Vertical.

(FIG. 84.)

The peculiar character of this gesture distinguishes it from the pointing gestures just described. It is used in Cautioning, Solemn Warning, and Threatening.

In Rogers' description of Genevra's picture we have it illustrated:

" She sits inclining forward as to speak,
   Her lips half open, and her finger up,
   As though she said, ' BEWARE! ' "

This mode of expression is specially appropriate in sacred discourse.

FIG. 84.

Ex.—1. STAND IN AWE and sin not.
sus.

2. VENGEANCE IS MINE; I will repay, saith the Lord.
sus.

Clinched Hand.

(FIG. 85.)

I. Used in any line for Extreme Emphasis, Vehement Declaration, Fierce Determination, Desperate Resolve. Often used in very emphatic assertion.

We have three degrees of emphasis: the open hand, the

FIG. 85.

index finger, the clinched hand; which may be denominated respectively Emphasis, Special Emphasis, and Extreme Emphasis.

Ex.— 1. Treason has done his WORST.
d. f. cli.

2. Let us do or DIE.
d. f. cli.

3. And when we have resisted to the *last*, we will STARVE in the
r. h. d. o. s.   d. f. cli.
wastes of the glaciers. Ay, men, women and *children*, we will
b. h. h. o.
all be frozen into ANNIHILATION together ere one free Switzer
b. h. d. o. cli.
will acknowledge a foreign MASTER.
r. h. h. o. cli.

4. I 'll have my BOND : I will not *hear* thee speak ;
r. h. d. f. cli.   r. h. d. l. p.
I 'll have my BOND, and therefore speak *no more*.
r. h. d. f. cli.   r. h. d. l. p.

The following example presents in their order the three degrees of emphasis above referred to:

To such usurpation I will never *submit ;* I repeat it, sir, I will
d. f. s.
never submit; I will DIE first.
d. f. ind.   d. f. cli.

7

The more usual method, however, in such cases, is to limit the action to one of these forms—the open hand, the index finger, or the clinched hand—and effect the climax by raising the hand higher and bringing it down more forcibly with each successive stroke.

II. The clinched hand is used in any line to express Violent Anger, Threatening, Defiance, etc.

Ex.—1. Wo to the hand that fails to rear,
　　　r. h. a. f. cli.
　　　At this dread sign, the ready spear.
　　　　　　　　　　　　　sus.

2. As a Roman, here in your very *capital* I DEFY you.
　　　　　　　　　　　h. f. ind.　h. f. cli.

3. Thy threats, thy mercies I DEFY,
　　　　　　　　　　　h. f. cli.
　　And give thee in thy *teeth* the lie.
　　　　　　　　　　h. f. ind.

4. If thou but FROWN on me, or stir thy FOOT,
　　　　　　h. f. cli.　　　　　　　　rep.
　　Or teach thy hasty spleen to do me SHAME,
　　I'll strike thee DEAD.　　　　　rep.
　　　　d. f. cli.

In more moderate discourse the idea of frowning might be expressed with the prone hand; but this would be inadequate to the vehemence of the present language.

III. Seizing, Grasping, etc.

Ex.—Then, starting from the ground once more, he SEIZED the monarch's
　　rein,　　*　　*　　*　　　　a. o. cli.
　　And with a fierce, o'er-mastering GRASP, the rearing war-horse led.
　　　　　　　　　　a. o. cli.

Both Hands Clinched.

This is admissible in Vehement Declaration and highly Impassioned Oratory.

Ex.—1. Rather than submit to such usurpation, I would suffer a THOUSAND
　　deaths.　　　　　　　　　　　b. h. d. f. cli.

2. I'll fight, till from my bones the FLESH be hack'd.
　　　　　　　　　　　b. h. d. l. cli.

Hands Applied.
(FIG. 86.)

The palms are pressed together as shown in the cut. Often used in Adoration.

Ex.—HOLY, holy, holy Lord God of Sabaoth.
　　b. h. a. f. ap.　　　　　　　　　　　　sus.

FIG. 86.　　　　　　　　FIG. 87.

Hands Clasped.
(FIG. 87.)

The hands are raised to the horizontal oblique, the palms facing each other, brought together and clasped, then drawn up to the chest, from which they are projected outward—descending, horizontal, or ascending— as occasion may require. In following this direction there need be no appearance of measured exactness; a fault which facility of execution must exclude from all gesture.

The clasped hands indicate strong emotion. They are appropriate in Supplication and Earnest Entreaty. Also the language of Distress.

Ex.—1. For HEAVEN's sake, Hubert, let me not be bound.
      b. h. h. f. cla.   sus.

2. O LORD, rebuke me not in Thy wrath.
   b. h. a. f. cla.

3. O ! my son ABSALOM ! my son, my son ABSALOM !   Would GOD
   b. h. h. f. cla.   rep.   b. h. a. f. cla.
I had died for THEE, O *Absalom*, my son, my *son*.
b. h. h. f. cla.   rep.   b. h. a. f. cla.   b. h. d. f. cla.

Hands Folded.
(FIG. 88.)

FIG. 88.

The fingers of the right hand are laid between the thumb and fore-finger of the left, the right thumb crossing the left.

Expressive of Humility or Self-Abasement, and sometimes employed in Sacred Address.

Ex.—Behold, I am vile !

Hands Crossed.
(FIG. 89.)

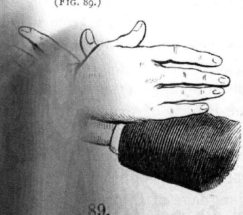

89.

One hand is placed upon the breast, and the other laid upon it. The eyes are at the same time slowly cast down, and the head bowed in Humility or Veneration.

Ex.—I acknowledge my transgression.

The Hand on the Heart.

Reference to the speaker's own feelings, and Impersonation as well, lays the hand on the heart. Powerful emotion presses it hard; fierce passion clinches it. In generous and genial emotions the fingers should be spread apart; in subdued emotions they are kept close together.

Ex.—1.　　　I feel within me
　　　A PEACE above all earthly dignities,
　　　A still and quiet CONSCIENCE.

2. Let my heart be STILL a moment and this mystery explore.

3. I speak from the fulness of my HEART.

4. Thou hast given to that poor, gentle, timid shepherd lad, *muscles*
　of iron and a heart of FLINT.　　　b. h. d. f. cli
　　　　　r. h. on heart cli.

Both hands are sometimes placed on the heart, one covering the other.

Ex.—What is this absorbs me quite;
　b. h. upl.
　Steals my senses, *shuts* my sight
　b. h. a. o. p.　　　b. h. h. l. p.
　DROWNS my spirit?
　b. h. on heart.

As a rule, the speaker in referring to the hearts of others, should not employ this gesture. In the following example, for instance,

They hushed their very hearts, that saw its horror and amaze.

The horizontal oblique prone is the most appropriate gesture.

The Left Hand.

The gestures assigned to the right hand may also be executed with the left, but only when absolutely necessary. As a rule, when one hand is employed singly, the preference should be given to the right. In referring to persons or objects at the left of the speaker, the left hand may be used. It should be remembered, however, that as an instrument of gesture, it is inferior, subordinate and occasional. Manly force prefers the right hand, which is, normally, the expressive hand; the left being a peculiarity and specialty. Its chief use is to accompany the right in expansion and warmth. To be constantly alternating between the right and left hand is a serious fault of gesture. There is, indeed, no necessity for it. In referring to the points of compass, the public speaker is not bound to give the exact directions. Upon this point, Austin says, "Avoid here literal and mechanical exactness." The contrast is all that can be required, and even in this he need not be punctilious. When a series of objects is presented, sufficient variety may be given by simply changing the lines of gesture; as when one member of the series is assigned to the line in front, a second to the oblique, a third to the lateral, and, it may be, a fourth to the oblique backwards; and this upon the descending, the horizontal, or the ascending plane. These divisions and subdivisions furnish the most ample scope for enumeration, classification and description. Observe the following notation:

Ex.—1. They shall come from the east, and from the WEST.
prea   r. h. h. l.

Or,

> They shall come from the east, and from the WEST.
> prep.   b. h. h. l.

Or, to be more specific:

> They shall come from the *east* and from the *west*.
>   r. h. h. f.   r.h.h.o.b.

2. He shall have dominion, also, from sea to SEA, and from the
prep.   r. h. h. l.

> river to the ENDS OF THE EARTH.
> prep.   b. h. h. l.

3. *Fear not*, for I am *with* thee; I will bring thy seed from the
r. h. h. l.   r. h. h. o.

> *east*, and gather thee from the *west;* I will say to the *north*
> r. h. h. l.   b. h. h. l. par. left.   r. h. h. f.
>
> give *up;* and to the *south*, keep not *back;* bring my sons
>   rep.   r. h. h. o. b.   r. h. d. o. b.
>
> from *far*, and my daughters from the *ends of the earth;* even
>   r. h. h. l.   r. h. h. o. b.
>
> *every one* that is called by my name.
> b. h. h. l.

4. Whatsoever thy hand findeth to *do*, do it with thy *might;* for there
                        h. o.   d. o.

> is no *work*, nor *device*, nor *knowledge*, nor *wisdom* in the *grave*
>   h. f.   d. o.   d. l.   d. o. b.   rep.
>
> whither thou goest.

5. If men of eminence are exposed to CENSURE on the one hand,
                           h. f.

> they are as much liable to FLATTERY on the other.
>   h. l.

Even in the last example the expression as notated is sufficiently definite. When more exactness is required, however, the left hand may be used singly; a practice never allowed by ancient orators, doubtless owing to the necessity of holding upon the left hand the folds of the toga, a cumbrous robe they were accustomed to wear.

CHAPTER X.

———

CONCLUSION.

Transition of Gesture.

In giving the elements of the subject it has been found most convenient to consider the hand at rest just previous to the execution of a given gesture; but in actual practice there are frequent transitions combining several different motions into a single period of gesture, as in the following notation:

No fearing, *no doubting* thy soldier shall know,
prep.　　　　　　　h. l.　　　　　　　　　　　　sus.
When *here* stands his country, and *yonder her foe;*
prep.　h. f.　　　　　　　sus.　prep.　h. l. ind.　sus.
One look at the bright *sun,* one prayer to the *sky,*
prep.　　　　　　　a. f.　　　prep.　　　b. h. a. o.
One glance where our *banner* waves glorious on high;
prep.　　　　　　　　　a. f. ind.
Then *on,* as the young lion bounds on his prey,
prep. b. h. h. f.　　　　　　　　　　　sus.
Let the sword flash on *high,* fling the scabbard *away;*
prep.　　　　　　a. o. ind.　　　　　　　　d. l.
Roll on, like the *thunderbolt* over the plain !
b. h. h. f.　　　　rep.　　　　　　　sus.
We come back in *glory,* or we come not *again.*
prep.　　　b. h. a. l.　prep.　　　b. h. d. o.

See illustrations on pages 258, 259, 260.

It will be observed here that the right hand does not fall to rest until the whole stanza is completed. Nor does it take the shortest line from one gesture to another, but first makes a new preparation, by being brought to a higher point, or a point nearer the body, from which it proceeds to the next position indicated in the notation. This new preparation may carry the hand to the head, or to a lower point; it may consist in a simple movement of the wrist.

The dotted line in fig. 90 corresponds with the line of preparation shown in fig. 6; the shorter curves are a series of preparations as applied to three successive gestures—d. o., h. o., and a. o.—in which the hand follows a line which successively returns upon itself.

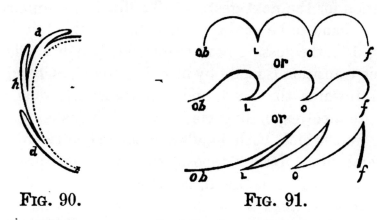

FIG. 90.   FIG. 91.

In fig. 91 the same principle is applied in the transverse direction. Observe that these lines, like those in fig. 90, are traced by one who faces the reader; hence they appear reversed. The lines will vary with the energy of the discourse. In tranquil delivery, the hand may pass from gesture to gesture by a simple curve, like that shown in the first diagram, fig. 91. The letters f. o. l. ob. represent the different terminations—front, oblique, lateral, and oblique backwards. The second diagram in the same figure shows a more graceful transition, in which the hand moves in double curves, similar to Hogarth's line of beauty. Such motions are

7*

adapted to a more elaborate oratorical style. The acute angles at the point of contact between the preparatory and executionary movements, as shown in the last diagram, are the result of more emphatic expression.

In making the transition from one hand to both, the left hand should be brought up from the place of rest simultaneously with the new preparatory movement performed by the right. In like manner, the transition from both hands to one is made by dropping the left hand at the same instant the right moves in preparation for the next gesture. To illustrate, suppose the right hand to be at the point h. l., and the left at rest (fig. 16), the gesture next required is b. h. h. l. (fig. 27). This transition is made by bringing the right hand from h. l. towards the head, and simultaneously raising the left to a corresponding elevation, as for instance, in fig. 71, from which both hands are carried outward to the lateral line. Now suppose the next gesture to be r. h. a. f. (fig. 18), the right hand is brought from h. l. towards the head while the left is falling to rest.

The Place of Gesture.

While it is obvious that the gesture occurs upon the emphatic word, it is well to consider its place with reference to the subject and predicate.

I. The gesture usually occurs upon the predicate, the subject taking the preparation.

Ex.—1. Our aim is HAPPINESS.
                h. o.
    2. The quality of mercy is NOT STRAINED.
                        h. l.

II. The subject takes the gesture when it is more important than the predicate.

Ex.—The ENTIRE RESOURCES OF THE GOVERNMENT were brought into
       b. h. h. l.
requisition.

III. When the subject and predicate are sufficiently important, a gesture may occur upon each.

Ex.—The voice of the LIVING speaker makes an impression on the mind
           h. o.
much STRONGER than can be made by the perusal of any WRITING.
   d. o.   rep.

IV. Of two or more subjects or predicates, the gesture generally falls upon the last.

Ex.—Truth, honor JUSTICE, were his motives.
             h. o.

V. A gesture may be made upon each of several subjects or predicates when they are sufficiently important, or when accompanied by strong qualifying words.

Ex.—The cloud-capt TOWERS, the gorgeous PALACES,
      b. h. a. f.   b. h. a. o.
The solemn TEMPLES, the great globe ITSELF,
      b. h. upl. a. o.   b. h. h. l.
Yea, all which it INHABIT shall DISSOLVE,
         imp.   b. h. d. l. p.
And like this insubstantial PAGEANT faded,
                r. h. h. l. p.
Leave not a WRECK behind.
       drop.

It is sometimes advantageous, instead of a gesture upon each member of a series—words, clauses or sentences—to alternate between them, assigning the preparation to the intervening members.

Ex.—1. To ARMS! they COME! the GREEK! the GREEK!
    b. h. h. f.   b. h. h. l. par.   prep.   b. h. h. l. par.

   2. The battle, sir, is not to the STRONG alone; it is to the VIGILENT,
     the active, the BRAVE.   h. l.   h. o.
     prep.   d. o.

   3. Now if any man build upon this foundation GOLD, silver,
                                    d. f.   prep.
     PRECIOUS STONES, WOOD, hay, STUBBLE, every man's work
     d. o.   d. l. prep.   d. o. b.   prep.
     shall be made MANIFEST.
           d. o.

With respect to the grammatical construction, the gesture most frequently occurs either upon the substantive or the verb, or else upon the adjective belonging to the former, or the adverb modifying the latter.

Ex.—1. ADVERSITY is the school of PIETY.
　　　　　h. o.　　　　　　　　　　　　　d. o.

　　　2. The true spirit of religion CHEERS as well as COMPOSES the soul.
　　　　　　　　　　　　　　　　　h. o.　　　　　　　　d. o.

　　　3. Exercise and temperance strengthen even an INDIFFERENT con-
　　　　　stitution.　　　　　　　　　　　　　　　　d. o.

　　　4. To love WISELY, rationally and PRUDENTLY, is, in the opinion
　　　　　prep.　　h. f.　　prep.　　　　　　h. o.
　　　　　of lovers, not to love AT ALL.
　　　　　　　　　　　　　　d. o.

The gesture often occurs upon the pronoun.

Ex.—Whom say YE that I am?
　　　　　　　　h. o.

Sometimes upon the interjection.

Ex.—These were *delightful* days, but ALAS ! they are no more.
　　　　　　　h. o.　　　　　　　r. h. upl.　　　　drop.

Climax.

Corresponding with the rhetorical climax, we have climax in gesture. By the law of force, gesture goes progressively inward and downward; by the law of feeling and expansion, progressively outward and upward. The orator should obey the law of climax in gesture, as well as in composition and voice. Indeed, these are but the constituent parts of the unity of effect, and should, therefore, harmonize with each other, as well as with the general character of the discourse and the circumstances of delivery.

In accordance with the law of climax, the elocutionist will economize voice and action, as the rhetorician economizes words. As the one reserves his strongest terms for the most important ideas, so will the other reserve his most forcible tones and gestures for the most emphatic assertions.

The following examples will serve to illustrate, in this connection, the principles which should govern in the choice of gesture:

Climax of Force.

Ex.—1. I *will* not, *must* not, *dare* not grant your wish.
　　r. h. d. l.　r. h. d. o.　r. h. d. f.

2. These abominable *principles*, and this more abominable *avowal*
　　　　　r. h. h. o.　　　　　　　　　r. h. d. o.
　of them, demand the most decisive *indignation*.
　　　　　　　　　　　　r. h. d. f.

3. I have very little *regard* for the assertion of my opponent ; it is
　　　　　　r. h. h. l.
　without *foundation ;* it is *false ; utterly* false.
　　r. h. d. l.　　　　r. h. d. o.　r. h. d. f.

4. They are all gone out of the *way ;* they are together become
　　　　　　　　　　r. h. h. l.
　unprofitable ; there is *none* that doeth good ; no, not *one.*
　　r. h. d. l.　　　　　r. h. d. o.　　　　　r. h. d. f.

Expansion.

5. For the truth of this assertion, I appeal to *you*, Mr. Chairman ;
　　　　　　　　　　　　r. h. h. f.
　I appeal to this *audience ;* yea, to the whole *world.*
　　　　b. h. h. o.　　　　　　　b. h. h. l.

6. Vanity of *vanities*, saith the preacher, vanity of *vanities ; all is*
　vanity.　r. h. d. l.　　　　　　　　　b.h.d.o.　b.h.d.l.

To use but one hand upon the last clause of this passage, after having used both hands in the preceding clause, would make an anti-climax, and weaken the effect of the action.

7. *Wave*, Munich ! *all* thy banners wave.
　r. h. h. l.　　　b. h. h. l.

8. Declare His glory among the *heathen*, His wonders among *all*
　the people.　　　b. h. h. o.　　　　　b. h. h. l.

9. Jehovah *reigns ;* His throne is *high ;*
      r. h. a. f.   r. h. a. o.
   His robes are light and *majesty.*
                           b. h. a. l.

10. He telleth the number of the *stars ;* He calleth them all by
      their *names.*   r. h. a. l.
         b. h. a. l.

11. *Great* is our Lord, and of great *power ;* His understanding is
      b. h. a. f.   b. h. a. o.
      infinite.
      b. h. a. l.

12. Be glad in the *Lord,* and *rejoice,* ye righteous ; and *shout* for joy,
         b. h. a. f.   b. h. a. o.   b. h. a. l.
   all ye that are upright in heart.

Elevation.

13. *Brief, brave* and *glorious* was his young career.
      r.h.d.f.   r.h.h.f   r. h. a. o.

14. According to the eternal rules of celestial precedency, Virtue
      takes place of *all* things.   It is the nobility of *Angels !*   It is
                     b. h. d. o.   b. h. a. o.
   the majesty of *God !*
      b. h. a. f.

The Rhetoric of Gesture.

Attention has already been called to the correspond-
ence between gesture and rhetoric.   The climax and
the rhetorical pause have been noticed.   Gesture is also
governed by the rhetorical figure.

Ex.—Thou art clothed with *light* as with a garment.
                           b. h. a. f. p.

The prone hands are here preferred, as being suggestive of apparel.   "Thou dwellest in light," would be
expressed with the supine hands.   So closely allied are
the two arts—construction and delivery—that the style
of rhetoric must govern the gesture generally.   Imper-
ative and vivid styles demand frequent and forcible
action, and *vice versa.*   Indeed, the rhetoric of gesture
should be carefully attended to.   As a rule, gestures

should be connected and harmonious. Appropriate and graceful action does not consist in isolated movements; the hand must not be allowed to drop after each emphatic word. On the contrary, the different movements should sustain such a relation to each other as to produce a good effect on the whole. Harmony and unity are essential elements of grace. Familiarity with this branch of the subject will lead to the arrangement of sentences with reference to the best effect in rhetorical delivery.

Gesture Modified by Circumstances.

The style of gesture to be adopted in a given case must be determined by the predominant idea, or the effect desired. If, in the following passage,

> I hate and abhor lying,

the speaker wishes simply to make an emphatic assertion, he will use the descending oblique; if he would indicate the class to which the object of his hatred belongs, he will employ the descending lateral— the gesture of debasement; if, however, the feeling of abhorrence be such as to call for a gesture of intense aversion, the descending oblique backwards prone would be appropriate. Take the same example in connection with its context:

> I hate and *abhor* lying; but Thy law do I *love*.
>   r h. h. l. v.   b. h. h. f.

The contrast here presented is better expressed with still another style of gesture, as shown in the notation. The idea which the hand expresses in this case is the putting away of one thing and the choosing of another in its stead.

In the last line of Bernardo del Carpio,

His banner led the spears no more amid the hills of Spain,

one might wish to indicate, with the pointing finger, the location of the hills of Spain, or treat the sentence as an unemphatic negation, and employ the horizontal lateral, or he might prefer to use the gesture of cessation—descending lateral—to express the termination of the young warrior's career.

Take the following couplet:

And will you rend our ancient love *asunder*,
b. h. h. o. s.
To join with men in *scorning* your poor friend?
b. h. d. o. s.

In choosing the gesture for this passage, the idea of earnest interrogation must predominate over that of disruption in the first line, and aversion in the second. Hence, instead of b. h. h. l. v., and r. h. d. l. p., we have the notation given above.

Compare the following examples:

1. *Bursts* the wild cry of terror and dismay.
b. h. a. l. v.

2. See through this air, this ocean, and this earth,
All matter quick and *bursting* into birth.
b. h. h. l. s.

In the first example the prevailing idea is that of disruption; in the second it is that of birth: and these must govern respectively the character of the gestures, which, although occurring upon like words, differ essentially in form and signification.

As the language of appeal, the following sentence would require the horizontal oblique:

Shall we now contaminate our fingers with base bribes?

But the force and depth of the emotion of contempt

absorbs the idea of appeal, and expresses itself with the descending lateral—both hands.

Victory and triumph usually find their appropriate expression in the ascending gestures; and yet, in the following couplet:

> The saints in all this glorious war
> Shall *conquer* though they *die*,
>   d. o.   rep.

the emphatic character of the language carries the hand to the descending line.

The elevation and expansion of feeling which constitute the emotion of joy, generally call for the ascending lateral; but the following sentence:

> A thing of beauty is a joy forever,

may be simply treated as the presentation of a general thought, and use the horizontal oblique. Observe here the distinction between the subjective and the objective —the inward excitement of an emotion, and the mere talking about it. In oblique discourse, however, the speaker often assumes an emotion or passion. Notice also the following:

> Give every man thine *ear*; but few thy *voice*.
>   b. h. h. o.   r. h. h. o. ind.
> Take each man's *censure*; but reserve thy *judgment*.
>   b. h. d. o.   r. h. h. o. ind.

If this were regarded as purely didactic, the supine hand would be retained throughout; but the shrewd caution of Polonius makes the gesture of mere instruction give place to that of warning—index finger.

The orator needs carefully to guard against the violation of the principle just stated, never sacrificing the greater for the less, but always adopting that style of

action which is most effective; for instance, at the
moment when he wishes to carry his point by forcible
argumentation, he must not allow himself to sacrifice
emphasis for any minor effect, as when he steps aside
to indulge in some descriptive action. There are times
when he cannot afford a descriptive gesture; as there
are emergencies in which the military commander may
not stop to admire the beauties of the natural scenery
which chance to lie in his pathway, but, with impetuous
speed, must hasten forward to combat the enemy.

A gesture is sometimes modified by its relation to
other gestures, or by the combined effect of the action.
In the passage,

> The Lord bringeth the counsel of the heathen to *nought;* He
> makketh the devices of the people of none *effect.* ^{d. o.}
> d. l.

The first clause, taken independently, and with moderate emphasis, would employ the descending lateral to
express nonentity; but since another clause of similar
import is added, the oblique is appropriated to the first,
in order to reserve the lateral for the second.

In the following appeal,

> For the truth of this assertion, I appeal to these gentlemen *before*
> b. h. h. f.
> me, to *every one* in this vast assembly, yea to the impartial
> b. h. h. o.
> judgment of *all mankind.*
> b. h. h. l.

The first clause taken separately would use b. h. h. o.;
and the second, either by itself, or in connection with
the first, b. h. h. l.; but when the three are combined,
by the law of rhetorical climax in delivery the largest
gesture is reserved for the largest idea.

In accordance with the same principle, both hands

are occasionally employed merely to preserve the harmony of the action—the preceding or the following idea requiring the use of both hands. This, however, is by no means an invariable rule, since the sudden transition from one hand to both, and *vice versa*, is not only admissible, but is often very effective. Some examples of this may be seen in the pieces marked for practice.

The gesture should accord with the idea taken in its full extent. Notice the second gesture in the notation of the following passage:

> With *all thy getting*, get *understanding*.
> b. h. h. o.   b. h. d. o.

The last clause standing alone, would be adequately expressed with one hand, but taken in connection with the first, the idea is extended, and hence requires a larger gesture. This also preserves the harmony of the action, the first clause obviously requiring both hands.

Gesture is modified by individual character. What is becoming to one, may not be so to another. This remark applies to the frequency and variety, and to the manner of execution. Different modes of thought call for different modes of expression. The orator who seldom steps beyond the bounds of calm reasoning, will confine himself chiefly to the class called assertive gestures, and will execute these with moderation; while one who is firm in his convictions, and possesses great strength of will, naturally lifts the hand higher and brings it down more forcibly; and one possessing a vivid imagination, will abound in descriptive gestures. Some physical organizations are more favorable to rhetorical action than others; pliability of muscle and

facility of motion generally will enable one to do what
would be quite unbecoming in another to attempt. Let
every one adopt that style of action which is best suited
to his own mental and physical organization, subject
always to the general laws of expression.

The Countenance.

The expression of the countenance is intimately
related to the subject of gesture. The mere motions
of the hands and arms without the appropriate facial
expression, and, indeed, without the appropriate attitude
and movement of the whole body, would result in
mechanical delivery void of grace or naturalness. The
face is a powerful auxiliary to the oratorical art. " By
the countenance," says Quintilian, " every feeling is
expressed. Upon the countenance the hearers depend,
and into it they examine before the speaker opens his
lips."

Says Lloyd:

> " The strongest passion bolts into the face."

And the same author thus describes the expression
of the countenance:

> " A single look more marks the internal woe,
>   Than all the windings of the lengthened o—h!
>   Up to the face the quick sensation flies,
>   And darts its meaning from the speaking eyes;
>   Love, transport, madness, anger, scorn, despair,
>   And all the passions, all the soul is there."

Lavater's observations upon the countenance are
valuable to the student of oratory. He makes the following distinction between physiognomy and pathognomy: " Physiognomy," he says, " is the knowledge of

the signs of the powers and inclinations of men. Pathognomy is the knowledge of the signs of the passions. Physiognomy, therefore, teaches the knowledge of the character at rest, and pathognomy, of the character in motion. All people read the countenance pathognomically (hence the expression of countenance necessary to the orator), few indeed read it physiognomically."

It is not the design of the present work to embrace a treatise upon facial expression. Some directions regarding the eyes, however, are indispensable to the study of gesture.

Among the three forms of visible expression—features, attitude and gesture—the eye occupies a prominent position. " It seems to share every emotion, and to belong to the soul more than any other feature." The expressive power of the eye is wonderful. The faculty—natural or acquired—of seizing an audience, so to speak, with the eye, and holding them in a visional grasp, endows the orator with marvelous power.

As a rule, the eye should not accompany the gesture, but should embrace the audience, traversing from left to right, beginning with those nearest the speaker, and going back to the farthest part of the house.

In impassioned poetry, the eye frequently accompanies the gesture ; so also in vivid description.

Apostrophic address turns toward its object.

In special designation the eye may for an instant glance toward the object pointed out. The rule in such cases is, that in vivid emotion the eye should precede the hand ; in moderate emotion they move simultaneously. To look the audience in the face while pointing them to a distant object, makes the truest eloquence. This, however, is not opposed to the momentary glance just referred to, and which heightens the effect.

In narrative and didactic discourse, as well as in all warm, earnest and vivid address, the eye, for the most part, ranges over the audience.

In strong resolve or fixed purpose, or in the statement of a definite proposition, it is fixed.

In intense emotion of a grand, solemn, or sublime character, when expressive of steadfastness, the eyes should remain fixed.

In profound solemnity and awe, they are upraised and fixed.

In shame or grief, they are downcast or averted.

In thought, they are cast on vacancy.

In doubt and anxiety, they turn in various directions.

The public reader should occasionally direct his eyes from the book or manuscript to the audience.

It may appear to some that so much attention to the details of gesture as is recommended in this treatise is unnecessary or impracticable; that it will hinder the freedom of action, or interfere with the fluency of speech, or draw the mind of the speaker from his subject matter, or allure him from the main purpose of his discourse, or cause the hearer to observe the manner more than the matter. It may be well to remind those who imagine all or any of these objections, that the same attention is necessary in the acquisition of every other branch pertaining to public speaking; that the orator is expected to frame his arguments with reference to the established rules of logic, arrange his thoughts according to the laws of rhetoric, construct his sentences with due regard to their grammatical government and agreement, give to every word its just pronounciation, and even to each letter its proper sound and full value; and that all these details are attended to during the most rapid utterance, and even in the vehemence of impassioned delivery, where the mind is entirely engrossed with the subject matter of the discourse, and the whole soul absorbed in the effort to accomplish the main purpose, whether it be to instruct, to convince, or to persuade; and, furthermore, that during the entire discourse neither speaker nor hearer gives a moment's thought to the rules of logic, rhetoric, or grammar. And why should not the rules of elocution, including both voice and gesture, be added to the list, and observed in the same manner?

MISCELLANEOUS EXAMPLES.

I.

I 've seen the moon climb the *mountain's* brow,
a. o. ind.
I 've watched the mists *o'er the river stealing;*
h. l. p.
But ne'er did I feel in my *breast* till *now,*
h. on heart.
So *deep,* so *calm,* and so *holy* a feeling:
rep.   rep.   a. o.
'T is soft as the thrill which memory throws
Athwart the *soul* in the hour of *repose.*
h. l. p.   d. l.

II.

His *throne* is on the *mountain* top,
a. o. ind.   rep.
  His *field* the *boundless air,*
  b. h. h. o.   b. h. h. l.
And *hoary hills* that proudly prop
  b. h. a. o.
  The *skies,* his *dwellings* are.
  b. h. a. l.   b. h. a. o.

III.

I am the Rider of the *wind,*
h. f.
  The Stirrer of the *storm!*
a. o.
The hurricane I left *behind*
h. l.
  Is yet with *lightning* warm;
a. l. ind.

8

To *speed* to thee, o'er shore and *sea*,
b. h. h. f.   b, h. h. o.
I swept upon the *blast*.
b. h. a. o.

IV.

Fill the bright *goblet, spread the festive board :*
h. f.   h. l.
Summon the *gay*, the noble and the *fair !*
b. h. h. f.   prep.   b. h. h. l.

V.

O ! *sweet* and beautiful is *night*,
b. h. upl.*   b. h. a. o.
When the silver *moon* is high,
a. o. ind.
And countless *stars* like glittering gems
b. h. a. o.
Hang *sparkling* in the sky ;
rep.
While the balmy breath of the summer *breeze*
b. h. h. f.
Comes whispering down the *glen ;*
b. h. d. f.
And one fond voice *alone* is heard,
h. o. ind.
O ! night is *lovely* then.
b. h. upl.   b. h. h. o.

VI.

Sullen, methinks, and slow the *morning breaks*,
a. l. v.
As if the sun were *listless* to appear,
rep.
And dark designs *hang heavy* on the day.
b. h. h. o. p.

VII.

Night *wanes*—the vapors round the *mountains* curl'd
h. l. p.   b. h. a. l. p.
Melt into morn, and *light awakes the world*.
b. h. h. l. p.   b. h. a. l.
How sweet and *soothing* is this hour of calm !
b. h. upl. a. o.   b. h. h. o. p.   eyes upl.

---

* Reference to the uplifted hand, unless otherwise designated, is to be understood vertical, as on pages 122, 125.

VIII.

How vain are all *hereditary honors*,
h. l.
Those poor possessions from *another's* deeds,
d. l.
Unless our *own just virtues* form our title,
b. h. h. o.
And give a *sanction* to our fond assumptions.
b. h. d. o.

IX.

And what is *most commended* at this time,
b. h. h. o.
Succeeding ages may account a *crime!*
b. h. d. o.

X.

The soul, of origin *divine*,
a. o.
  God's glorious image, *freed from clay*,
  a. f.   h. l.
In *heaven's eternal sphere* shall shine
  b. h. a. l.
  A *star of day!*
  a. o. ind.
The *sun* is but a *spark of fire*,
  a. f.   a. l. ind.
  A *transient meteor* in the sky;
  a. l.
The *soul* immortal as its *sire*,
  a. o. ind.   a. f. ind.
  Shall *never* die.
  d. o. ind.

XI.

The stars shall *fade away*, the sun himself grow dim with age,
b. h. a. o. v.
and nature *sink* in years; but this shall flourish in immortal *youth*,
b. h. d. l. p.   a. o.
unhurt amid the war of *elements*, the wreck of matter and the *crash*
b. h. a. o.   b. h. h. l.
of worlds.

XII.

Are you an *actor* in this busy scene, or are you an idle *spectator?*
h. f.   h. l.

XIII.

War! War!—aloud with *general voice* they cry.
b. h. h. o. rep.   b. h. h. l.

XIV.

Thou *tremblest*, and the whiteness in thy *cheek* .
     h. f. p.   h. f.
Is apter than thy *tongue* to tell thy errand.
          rep.

XV.

Hence! home! you idle creatures, get you *home!*
h. o. v. h. l. v.   h. o. b. v.

XVI.

Take holy earth, all that my soul holds *dear.*
b. h. d. f.   rep.

XVII.

The *Grave, dread thing!*
     d. f. p. a. f. v. (eyes upraised.)
Men *shiver* when thou 'rt named: Nature *appall'd*,
   b. h. d. o.   b. h. upl. a. o.
Shakes off her wonted firmness. Ah! how *dark*
b. h. d. l. p.   b. h. a. o. p.
Thy long-extended *realms*, and rueful *wastes!*
     b. h. h. l. p.   b. h. d. l. p.
Where nought but *silence* reigns, and night, *dark night,*
     b. h. upl. a. o.   b. h. h. l. p.
Dark as was *Chaos*, ere the infant *Sun*
    b. h. upl. a. o.   a. f. ind.
Was rolled together, or had tried his beams
Athwart the *gloom profound.* The sickly *taper,*
      b. h. a. f.   ·   h. f. ind.
By glimm'ring through thy low-brow'd misty *vaults,*
            b. h. d. f.
Furr'd round with mouldy damps, and ropy *slime,*
--- b. h. d. l. p.
Lets fall a *supernumerary horror,*
     b. h. upl. a. o.
And only serves to make thy night *more irksome.*
          b. h. h. o. p.

XVIII.

I could a tale unfold, whose *lightest word*
h. o. ind.

Would harrow up thy *soul, freeze* thy blood,
h. f. ind. d. f.

Make thy two eyes, like stars, *start from their spheres,*
b. h. h. l. very quick.

Thy knotted and combined locks to *part,*
b. h. d. o.

And each particular *hair* to stand on *end,*
h. o. ind.   rep.

Like quills upon the fretful *porcupine.*
h. l. ind.

XIX.

The temples of the *gods*, the gods *themselves*, will *justify* the cry,
b. h. a. o.   rep.   b. h. d. o.

and *swell* the general sound, *Revenge !* Revenge ! *Revenge !*
b. h. h. l.   d. o. cli.   prep.   rep.

XX.

—— We 've sworn by our country's *assaulters,*
h. l. cli.

By the virgins they 've dragged from our *altars,*
b. h. d. l. par.

By our massacred *patriots*, our children in *chains,*
    b. h. h. o.   b. h. d. o.

By our heroes of *old* and their blood in our *veins,*
    h. o. b.   b. h. d. o. cli.

That living, we will be *victorious,*
a. o. cli.

Or that *dying,* our deaths shall be *glorious.*
   b. h. d. f. cli.   b. h. a. o.

XXI.

The physical *universe* may be regarded as exhibiting, at once, all
h. o.

its splendid *varieties* of events, and *uniting,* as it were, in a single
b. h. a. o.   b. h. h. f.

moment, the wonders of *eternity. Combine,* by your *imagination,* all
rep.   b. h. a. l.   b. h. h. o.   rep.

the fairest *appearances* of things. Suppose that you see, at *once,* all the
b. h. h. l.   b. h. h. f.

hours of the *day,* and all the seasons of the *year ;* a morning of *spring*
b. h. h. o.   b. h. h. l.   b. h. h. o.

and a morning of *autumn*, a night brilliant with *stars*, and a night
b. h. d. o.   b. h. a. o.

obscure with *clouds ;* meadows enamelled with *flowers ;* fields waving
b. h. a. o. p.   b. h. d. f.

with *harvests ;* woods, heavy with the frosts of *winter :* you will then
b. h. h. o.   b. h. h. l. p.

have a just notion of the spectacle of the *universe.*
b. h. h. l.

XXII.

I am charged with pride and *ambition.*   The charge is *true*, and I
h. o.   d. l.

glory in its truth.   Whoever achieved anything great in *letters*, arts
a. o.   h. o.

or *arms* who was *not* ambitious?   *Cæsar* was not more ambitious than
h. l.   imp.   h. f.

Cicero : it was but in another *way.*   Let the ambition be a *noble* one,
h. l.   d. l.   a. o.

and who shall *blame* it?
h. o.

XXIII.

The greatest glory of a *free-born people*,
b. h. h. o.

Is to transmit that freedom to their *children.*
b. h. d. o.

XXIV.

Mr. *Chairman*, I call on your interference to put a *stop* to this
h. f.   d. f.

uproar.

XXV.

Such, where ye find, *seize fast*, and *hither* bring.
h. o.   h. o. p.   d. o.

XXVI.

The great *King of kings*
h. o. ind.

Hath in the table of His law *commanded*,
h. f. ind.

That thou shalt do *no murder ;* wilt thou then
d. o. ind.

Spurn at His edict, and fulfil a *man's ?*
d. l.   d. o.

XXVII.

I died no *felon death* —
d. l.

A *warrior's weapon* freed a *warrior's soul.*
h. o. h. l.

XXVIII.

Peace is *despair'd,*
d. l.

For who can *think submission!* *War,* then, *war*
d. o. h. f. rep.

Open or understood, must be *resolved.*
d. f.

XXIX.

'T is not in *mortals* to *command* success;
d. o. rep.

But we 'll do *more,* Sempronius, we 'll *deserve* it.
b. h. d. o. rep.

XXX.

Speak of a man as *you* find him,
h. f.

And heed not what *others* may say.
h. l.

XXXI.

Can ministers still presume to expect *support* in their infatuation?
h. o.

Can *Parliament* be so dead to its dignity and duty, as to *give* its sup-
b. h. h. o. b. h. d. o.

port to measures thus intruded and *forced* upon it?
b. h. d. f.

XXXII.

Vain hopes and *empty joys* of human kind,
d. o. d. l.

Proud of the *present,* to the future *blind.*
h. f. h. o. p.

XXXIII.

Thus pleasures *fade away,*
h. l.

Youth, talents, beauty, thus decay,
d. l. ----------------

And leave us *dark,* forlorn, and *grey.*
r. h. upl. d. l.

XXXIV.

When *beauty* triumphs, ah *beware !*
    h. o.   h. o. ind.
Her smile is *hope !* her frown *despair !*
         a. f.   d. f.

XXXV.

Who that surveys this *span of earth* we press,
                 b. h. d. o.
This *speck* of life in time's great *wilderness,*
 d. f. ind.   b. h. h. l.
This narrow *isthmus* 'twixt *two boundless seas,*
          d. f.   b. h. h. l.
The *past,* the *future,* two *eternities !*
  h. o. b.   h. f.   b. h. a. l.
Would *sully* the bright spot or leave it *bare,*
  d. f. p.   d. l.
When he might ·build him a proud *temple* there,
                 b. h. a. o.
A name, that long shall hallow *all its space,*
                 b. h. a. l.
And be each purer soul's high *resting place.*
                 b. h. a. f.

XXXVI.

How can it enter the thoughts of man that the *soul,* which is
h. o.   h. f.
capable of such immense *perfections,* and of receiving new improve-
                    a. o.
ments to *all eternity,* shall fall away into *nothing* almost as soon as
       a. l.   d. o.
created.
d. l.

XXXVII.

Our thoughts are *boundless,* though our frames are *frail,*
          b. h. h. l.   b. h. d. o.
Our souls *immortal,* though our limbs *decay ;*
       b. h. a. o.   b. h. d. l.
Though *darken'd* in this poor life by a veil
   h. o. p.
Of suffering, dying *matter,* we shall play
         b. h. d. l. p.
In truth's eternal *sunbeams ;* on the way
        b. h. a. o.

To Heaven's high *capitol* our cars shall roll ;
b. h. a. f.
The temple of the Power whom *all obey*,
b. h. d. o.
That is the mark we tend to, for the soul
a. f. ind.
Can take *no lower* flight, and seek *no meaner* goal.
d. o.   d. l.

XXXVIII.

See through *this air*, *this ocean, and this earth*,
b. h. h. l.
All matter *quick*, and *bursting* into birth.
b. h. h. o.   b. h. h. l.
Above, how *high !* progressive life may go !
b. h. a. f.
Around, how *wide !* how *deep* extend *below !*
b. h. h. l.   b. h. d. f.   rep.
Vast chain of being ! which from *God* began,
b. h. h. l.   a. f.
Nature's ethereal, human, angel, *man*,
h. f.
Beast, bird, fish, insect, what *no eye* can see,
h. l.   d. l.
No glass can *reach*, from *infinite* to *thee*,
h. l.   imp.   b. h. a. l.   h. f.
From *thee* to *nothing*.
h. f.   d. l.

XXXIX.

From *cloud to cloud* the *rending lightnings rage ;*
b. h. a. o. v.   b. h. a. l. v.
Till, in the furious elemental war
Dissolv'd, the whole precipitated mass
b. h. a. l. v.
Unbroken *floods* and solid *torrents* pour.
b. h. h. o. p.   b. h. d. o.

XL.*

I went by the *field of the slothful*, and by the *vineyard of the man*
h. o.
void of understanding ; and *lo*, it was all grown over with *thorns*, and
h. l.   h. l. ind.   d. o. p.

---

* While the Scriptures and sacred hymns are here used for illustration, it is not with a view of recommending the employment of gesture in their public reading ; but only when they are quoted by the public speaker, and form a part of the discourse.

nettles had covered the face thereof, and the stone wall thereof was
d. l. p.

broken down.   Then I saw and *considered it well :* I looked upon it,
d. o. b. p.   d. f. ind.

and received *instruction.*   Yet a little *sleep,* a little *slumber,* a little
rep.   d. f.   d. o.

folding of the hands to sleep : so shall thy *poverty* come as one that
hands folded.   h. f. ind.

travaileth ; and thy *want* as an *armed man.*
h. l. ind.   h. o.   d. o. ind.

XLI.

They cried unto the *Lord* in their trouble, and He delivered them
b. h. a. f.

out of their *distresses.*
b. h. d. l.

XLII.

Were the whole realm of *nature* mine,
b. h. h. l.

That were a present far too *small ;*
b. h. d. o.

Love so *amazing,* so *divine,*
b. h. upl. a. o.   b. h. a. f.

Demands my *soul,* my *life,* my *all.*
b. h. h. f.   b. h. d. o.   b. h. d. l.

XLIII.

He who reigns on high

Upholds the *earth,* and spreads abroad the *sky,*
b. h. h. f.   b. h. a. l.

With *none* His name and power will He divide,
d. f.

For He is *God* and there is *none* beside.
a f.   d. l.

XLIV.

It chills my *blood* to hear the blest Supreme
b. h. d. f.

Rudely appealed to on each trifling theme ;
b. h. d. o.

Maintain your *rank,* vulgarity *despise,*
d. f.   d. l.

To swear is neither *brave, polite,* nor *wise ;*
d. f.   d. o.   d. l.

You would not swear upon a bed of *death !*
                                        d. f.

Beware ! your Maker *now* may stop your breath.
h. o. ind.   d. f. ind.

XLV.

A *scorner* seeketh *wisdom,* and findeth it *not :* but knowledge is
h. o. ind.   h. o.   d. o.

easy unto him that understandeth.
d. l.

XLVI.

The getting of treasure by a *lying tongue* is a vanity tossed *to and*
                                h. o.   h. l.

fro of them that seek *death.*
                      d. o.

XLVII.

There is that maketh himself *rich,* yet hath *nothing :* there is that
                                h. o.   drop.

maketh himself *poor,* yet hath *great riches.*
               d. l.   b. h. d. o.

XLVIII.

I have rejoiced in the way of Thy *testimonies* as much as in *all*
                                      a. o.

riches.
b.h.h.o.

XLIX.

Better is a *little* with the fear of the Lord, than *great treasure* and
                   d. l.   h. l.

trouble therewith.
d. l.

L.

If thou hast done *foolishly* in *lifting up* thyself, or if thou hast
                      d. o.   a. o.

thought evil, lay thine *hand* upon thy mouth.
h. o.   h. f. p.

LI.

The Lord hath made all things for *Himself :* yea even the *wicked*
                             b. h. a. f.   b. h. d. f.

for the day of *evil.*
          rep.

LII.

The *dark* places of the earth are full of the habitations of *cruelty*.
h. l.   d. l.

LIII.

The Lord doth *build up* Jerusalem: He *gathereth together* the out-
         h. o.   b. h. h. o.
casts of Israel. He *healeth* the broken in heart, and *bindeth up* their
                h. o. p.   b. h. d. o.
wounds. He telleth the number of the *stars;* He calleth them all by
                                 a. l.
their *names*. *Great* is our Lord, and of great *power;* His understand-
     b. h. a. l. b. h. a. f.   b. h. a. o.
ing is *infinite*. The Lord lifteth up the *meek;* He casteth the wicked
   b. h. a. l.   h. o.
down to the ground.
  d. o. p.

LIV.

Open thy *mouth*, judge *righteously*, and *plead the cause* of the poor
        h. o.   d. o.   b. h. h. o.
and needy.

LV.

With the Lord there is *mercy*, and with Him is *plenteous redemption*.
          h. o.   b. h. h. l.
And He shall *redeem* Israel from all his *iniquities*.
    b. h. h. o.   b. h. d. o.

LVI.

The tongue of the *just* is *choice silver:* the *heart of the wicked* is
          h. o.   d. o.   h. l.
little worth.
  d. l.

LVII.

Faithful are the *wounds of a friend;* but the *kisses of an enemy*
  d. f.   h. f.   h. o.
are *deceitful*.
  d. l.

LVIII.

Rivers of waters run down mine eyes, because they keep not Thy
b. h. d. o.   drop.
law.

LIX.

My zeal hath *consumed* me, because mine enemies have *forgotten*
        b. h. d. f.   b. h. d. l.
Thy words.

LX.

Rejoice, O young man, in thy *youth ;* and let thy heart *cheer* thee
 h. f.   rep.   h. o.
in the days of thy youth, and walk in the ways of thine *heart* and in
                                       h. f.
the sight of thine *eyes :* but *know* thou, that for *all these things*
         h.o.   h. f. ind.   b. h. h. o.
God will bring thee into judgment.
r. h. upl. ind.   sus.

LXI.

A' *friend* cannot be known in *prosperity*, and an *enemy* cannot be
 h. o.   h. l.   d. o.
hidden in *adversity.*
     d. l.

LXII.

There is not a just man upon *earth*, that doeth good and *sinneth*
                  d. o.   d. l.
not.

LXIII.

Get wisdom, get *understanding : forget it not ;* neither *decline* from
 h f. ind.   h. o. ind.   rep.   d. o. ind.
the words of my mouth. *Forsake* her not, and she shall *preserve* thee ;
                 h. f. ind.   d. o.
love her, and she shall *keep* thee. *Wisdom* is the *principal* thing ;
h. f.   d. f.   h. o.   d. o.
therefore get *wisdom :* and with *all thy getting* get *understanding.*
         h. o.   b. h. h. o.   b. h. d. o.
Exalt her, and she shall *promote* thee : she shall bring thee to *honor,*
a. f.   a. o.   a. l.
when thou dost *embrace* her. She shall give to thine head an *orna-*
          h. o.   a. o.
ment of grace : a *crown of glory* shall she deliver to thee.
                a. l.

LXIV.

Without *counsel* purposes are *disappointed :* but in the *multitude* of
     h. o.   d. o.   b. h. h. o.
counsellors they are *established.*
            b. h. d. o.

LXV.

Commit thy works unto the *Lord*, and thy thoughts shall be *estab-*

a. f.   d. f.
lished.

LXVI.

There are many *devices* in a man's heart; nevertheless the counsel

h. o.
of the *Lord*, that shall *stand.*

a. f.   h. f.

LXVII.

He came unto His *own*, and His own *received Him not.*

b. h. h. f.   b. h. d. o.

LXVIII.

I have seen the wicked in *great power*, and spreading himself like

a. o.
a *green bay tree.* Yet he *passed away*, and lo, he *was not:* yea I

a. l.   h. l.   d. o. ind.
sought him, but he could not be *found.*

h. o.   d. l.

LXIX.

He that gathereth in *summer* is a *wise* son: but he that *sleepeth*

h. o.   d. o.   h. l.
in harvest is a son that causeth *shame.*

d. l.

LXX.

Except the *Lord* build the house, they labor in *vain* that build it.

a. f.   d. l.

LXXI.

The Lord will not *cast off* His people, neither will He *forsake* His

d. l.   h. l.
inheritance.

LXXII.

Blessings are upon the head of the *just;* but *violence* covereth the

b. h. h. o.   rep.   d. o. p.
mouth of the *wicked.*

rep.

LXXIII.

The *wise in heart* will receive *commandments :* but a *prating fool*
  h. o.   d. o.   h. l.
shall *fall.*
d. l.

LXXIV.

Beware of false *prophets*, which come to you in *sheep's clothing ;*
      h. o.   d. l.
but inwardly they are ravening *wolves.*
           d. f.

LXXV.

He that saith unto the *wicked*, thou art *righteous ;* him shall the
        h. o.   rep.
people *curse, nations* shall *abhor* him.
d. o. ind. h. l.   d. o. b.

LXXVI.

In all *labor* there is *profit :* but the talk of the *lips* tendeth only
  h. o.   d. o.   h. l.
to *poverty.*
d. l.

LXVII.

Hell and destruction are *never full ;* so the *eyes of man* are never
 b. h. d. o.   b. h. d. l.   b. h. h. o.
satisfied.
b. h. d. o.

LXXVIII.

Every prudent man dealeth with *knowledge :* but a fool layeth open
           h. o.
his *folly.*
d. l.

LXXIX.

As for *man*, his days are as *grass :* as a *flower of the field*, so he
  h. f.   d. f.   d. o.
flourisheth. For the wind *passeth over it*, and it is *gone ;* and the place
        d. l. p.   drop. no action.
thereof shall know it no more.

LXXX.

He hath remembered His covenant *for ever*, the word which He
             h. o.
commanded to a *thousand generations.*
     b. h. h. l.

LXXXI.

In the transgression of an *evil man* there is a *snare :* but the
h. o.   d. o.
righteous doth sing and *rejoice.*
h. f.   a. o.

LXXXII.

The poor and the deceitful man *meet* together: the Lord lighteneth
b. h. h. f
both their eyes.
b. h. h. o.

LXXXIII.

What shall it *profit* a man, if he shall gain the *whole world,* and
b. h. h. o.   b. h. h. l.
lose his *own soul?* Or what shall a man give in *exchange* for his soul?
b. h. d. l.   b. h. d. o.

LXXXIV.

Here mercy's boundless *ocean* flows,
b h. h. l.
To cleanse our guilt and heal our *woes;*
b. h. d. o.
Pardon and life and endless *peace,*
b. h. h. o.
How rich the *gift!* how *free* the grace!
b. h. upl. a. o. b. h. h. l.

LXXXV.

Tune your harps *anew,* ye seraphs;
b. h. a. o,
Join to sing the pleasing theme:
rep.
All in *earth* and *Heaven* uniting,
b. h. h. o.   b. h. a. o.
Join to praise *Immanuel's* name.
b. h. a. f.

LXXXVI.

There is a time, we know not *when,*
h o. p.
A point, we know not *where,*
h. l. p.
That marks the *destiny* of men,
h. o. ind.
To glory or *despair ;*
d. l. ind.

There is a line, by us *unseen*,
h. f. ind.
That crosses every *path*,
h. o. ind.
The hidden boundary between
God's *patience* and His *wrath*.
r. h. upl.   d. o.

LXXXVII.

The names of all His *saints* He bears,
b. h. a. o.
Deep graven on His *heart;*
b. h. a. f.
Nor shall the *meanest* Christian say
d. l.
That he hath *lost* his part.
drop.

Those *characters* shall fair abide,
b. h. a. o.
Our everlasting *trust*,
b. h. d. f.
When gems, and monuments, and *crowns*,
------------------------------ b. h. upl. a. o.
Are mouldered down to *dust*.
b. h. d. l. p.

LXXXVIII.

Now there are diversities of *gifts*, but the same *Spirit*.   And there
h. o.   a. o.
are differences of *administrations*, but the same *Lord*.   And there are
h. l.   h. f.
diversities of *operations*, but it is the same *God* which worketh *all in all*.
h. o.   a. f.   b. h. h. l.

LXXXIX.

Thy kingdom is an *everlasting* kingdom, and Thy dominion endureth
b. h. h. o.
throughout *all generations*.
b. h. h. l.

XC.

The eyes of the Lord are in *every place*, beholding the *evil and the*
b. h. h. l.
good.
rep.

XCI.

He clave the rocks in the *wilderness,* and gave them drink as out
                                    h. l.
of the *great depths.* He brought streams also out of the *rock,* and
        d. l.   b. h. h. f.
caused waters to run down like *rivers.*
                          b. h. d. f.

XCII.

Turn ye, *turn* ye, for *why* will ye die?
         b. h. h. f.   b. h. h. o.

XCIII.

And the *rain descended* and the *floods came,* and the *winds blew,* and
        b. h. a. f. p.   b. h. a. o. p.   b. h. a. l. p.
beat upon that house; and it *fell:* and *great* was the fall of it.
b. h. h. f. p.   b. h. d. o. p.   drop.

XCIV.

Who hath ascended up into *Heaven,* or *descended?* Who hath
h f.   a. f.   d. f.
gathered the *winds* in His fists? Who hath bound the *waters* in a
             a. o.   b. h. h. o.
garment? Who hath established *all the ends of the earth?*
                               b. h. h. l.

XCV.

O may I no longer dreaming,
  Idly *waste* my golden days;
       b. h. h. l. p.
But each precious hour *redeeming,*
                       h. o.
  Upward, onward, press my way.
  a. f.   b. h. h. f.

XCVI.

In thoughts from the visions of the *night,* when deep *sleep* falleth
                                    r. h. upl.   h. o. p.
on men, fear came upon me, and *trembling,* which made all my bones
                               r. h. upl. tremor.
to *shake.* Then a *spirit* passed before my face; the hair of my flesh
b. h. upl. tr.   h. f.
stood up: it stood *still,* but I could not *discern* the form thereof: an
r. h. upl.   h. f. p.   drop.

image was before mine eyes, there was *silence*, and I heard a voice,
h. f.   drop.
saying, Shall *mortal man* be more just than *God?* Shall a *man* be
d. o.   a. f.   h. l.
more pure than his *Maker?*
a. l.

XCVII.

The heathen are *sunk down* in the pit that they made ; in the net
d. o. p.
which they *hid* is their own *foot taken.*
b. h. d. o.   b. h. d. f.

XCVIII.

Let them all be *confounded* and turned *back* that hate Zion.
d. o. p.   d. l. p.

XCIX.

Zion *awake ;* thy strength *renew ;*
b. h. a. o.   b. h. h. o.
Put on thy robes of beauteous *hue ;*
b. h. a. o.
Church of our God, arise and *shine,*
b. h. a. l.
Bright with the beams of truth divine.

Soon shall thy radiance stream *afar,*
b. h. h. l.
Wide as the *heathen nations* are ;
imp.
Gentiles and kings thy light shall *view ;*
b. h. a. o.
All shall admire and love thee too.
b. h. a. l.

C.

Jerusalem is builded as a city that is *compact* together.
b. h. h. f.

CI.

Thy testimonies are *wonderful :* therefore my soul doth *keep* them.
b. h. a. o.   b. h. h. o.

CII.

Open Thou mine *eyes* that I may behold *wondrous* things out of
   b. h. a. o.   b. h. a. l.

Thy law.

CIII.

That which *hath been* is *now ;* and that which *is to be* hath *already*
    h. l.   h. f.   a. f.   d. f.

been ; and *God* requireth that which is *past.*
    a. f.   h. l.

CIV.

The Lord on high is mightier than the noise of *many waters*, yea
             b. h. h. o.

than the mighty waves of the *sea.*
        b. h. h. l.

CV.

The Lord is great, and greatly to be praised: He is to be feared
above *all* gods. For all the gods of the nations are *idols :* but the
  b. h. a. o.   d. l.

Lord made the *heavens.* Honor and *majesty* are before Him : strength
   b. h. a. o.   b. h. a. f.

and beauty are in His *sanctuary.* * * * O that men would
       b. h. h. o.

praise the Lord for His *goodness,* and for His wonderful *works* to the
        b. h. a. o.   b. h. h. o.

children of men.

CVI.

That which is *far off* and *exceeding deep,* who can *find it out ?*
    h. l.   b. h. d. f.   h. o.

CVII.

Amazing sight ! the *Saviour* stands
b. h. upl. a. o.   h. f. p.
  And knocks at every *door !*
       h. o. p.
  Ten thousand *blessings* in His hands,
     b. h. h. o.
  To satisfy the *poor.*
    d. h. d. o.

CVIII.

Enter ye in at the *strait* gate ; for *wide* is the gate, and *broad* is the
b. h. h. f. b. h. h. o. b. h. h. l.
way that leadeth to *destruction,* and *many* there be which go in thereat ·
b. h. d. o. b. h. d. l.
because *strait* is the gate and narrow is the way which leadeth unto
b. h. h. f.
life, and *few* there be that find it.
b. h. a. f. b. h. d. f.

CIX.

Enter not into the path of the *wicked,* and go not in the way of
h. f. ind.
evil men. *Avoid* it, *pass not* by it, turn *from* it, and *pass away.*
h. l. ind. h. l. p. h. l. ind. h. l. p. d. l. p.

CX.

When the *wicked are multiplied, transgression increaseth.*
b. h. h. o. b. h. d. o.

CXI.

A man's *pride* shall bring him *low :* but *honor* shall *uphold* the
h. o. d. o. a. o. rep.
humble in spirit.

CXII.

Boast not thyself of *to-morrow ;* for thou knowest not what a *day*
h. f. ind. d. o.
may bring forth.

CXIII.

Like *floods* the angry nations rise,
b.h.h.o.
And aim their rage against the *skies ;*
b.h.a.o.
Vain floods, that aim their rage so high ;
h. l.
At His rebuke the billows *die.*
d.l.p.

CXIV.

Hark! a brazen voice
r. h. upl. ind.
Swells from the *valley*, like the *clarion*
　　　　h. l. ind.　　　　　h. o. ind.
That calls to battle.

CXV.

This doctrine, as long as I have *breath*, I shall *oppose*.
h. f.　　　　　　　　　　rep.　　　　　　d. f.

CXVI.

It may be said that disease generally *begins* that equality which
　　　　　　　　　　　　　　　　h. o.
death *completes*.
d. o.

CXVII.

Clearness, force and *earnestness* are the qualities which produce
　　　　　　　　　　d. o.
conviction.

CXVIII.

Grace was in all her *steps*, *heaven* in her eye,
h. o.　　　　　　　imp.　　a. o.
In every gesture dignity and *love*.
　　　　　　　　　　　　d. o.

CXIX.

Know thou *this* truth (*enough* for man to know),
　　　h. f.　　　　　h. l.
Virtue *alone* is happiness.
　　　d. o.

CXX.

Begone, I will not *hear* thy vain excuse,
h. l. p.　　　　　d. l. p.
But as thou lov'st thy *life*, make *speed* from hence.
　　　　　　　　h. f. ind.　　　h. l.

CXXI.

Why should we count our life by *years*,
　　　　　　　　　　　h. o.
Since years are short and *pass away*.
　　　　　　　　　h. l.

CXXII.

I 've touch'd the *highest point* of all my greatness;

a. f. ind.

And from that full *meridian* of my glory,

a. f.

I haste now to my *setting*. I shall fall,

h. l. p.

Like a bright exhalation in the *evening;*

h. l. ind.

And no man see me more.

drop.

CXXIII.

All flesh is *grass*, and all its glory *fades*.

b.h.d.o.   b.h.d.l.

CXXIV.

And what is *friendship* but a *name*,

h. o.   h. l.

A charm that lulls to *sleep:*

d. l.

A shade that follows *wealth or fame*,

h. l.

And leaves the *wretch* to weep.

d. l.

CXXV.

Lighter than the *whirlwind's* blast,

a. l.

He *vanished* from our eyes.

drop.

CXXVI.

I had a *seeming friend;* I gave him *gifts*,

h. o.   h. l.

And he was *gone*.

drop.

CXXVII.

What is *glory?* What is *fame?*

a. o.   a. l.

The echo of a *long lost name*,

d. l. p.

A *breath*, an *idle hour's* brief talk;

h. l.   d. l.

A flower that blossoms for a *day*,
h. l.

Dying next morrow.
drop.

A stream that *hurries on its way*,
h. l.

Singing of sorrow.
drop.

CXXVIII.

Hail horrors! hail,
b. h. a. o.   rep.

Infernal world, and thou, *profoundest hell,*
b. h. h. o.   b. h. d. f.

Receive thy new possessor.
rep.

CXXIX.

Can you raise the *dead?*
d. f.

Pursue and overtake the *wings of time?*
a. o.

And bring about again the hours, the days,

The years *that made me happy!*
h. l.

CXXX.

Rise, fathers! *rise!* 't is *Rome* demands your help.
b. h. h. o.   b. h. a. o.   h. l.

CXXXI.

My heart is *withered* at that piteous sight.
r. h. on heart.

CXXXII.

The dying agonies of one who dies to *save* him,
d. f.

Excite no *sympathy* in his breast.
d. l.

CXXXIII.

Unnumber'd suppliants *crowd* preferment's gate,
b. h. h. o.   b. h. h. f.

Athirst for wealth, and *burning* to be great,
b. h. a. o.

Delusive *fortune* hears the incessant call,
r. h. h. l. ind.

They *mount*, they *shine*—*evaporate* and *fall.*
b. h. h. f.   b. h. a. o.   b. h. h. l.   drop.

CXXXIV.

Through many a *clime* 't is mine to go,

h. l.

With many a *retrospection* curst,

h. l. p.

And all my *solace* is to know,

h. o.

Whate'er betides, I 've known the *worst.*

h. l.   d. o.

What *is* the worst? Nay, *do not ask,*

h. f.   h. l. p.

In *pity* from the search *forbear :*

h. f p.   imp.

Smile on — nor venture to unmask

h. o.

Man's heart, and view the *hell* that 's there.

d. f.

CXXXV.

The quality of mercy is not *strain'd ;*

h. l.

It droppeth, as the gentle rain from *heaven,*

a. o.

Upon the place *beneath :* it is *twice* bless'd ;

d. o.   d. f.

It blesseth him that *gives,* and him that *takes :*

h. o.   d. o.

T is mightiest in the *mightiest ;* it becomes

a. o.

The throned *monarch* better than his *crown :*

a. l.   h. l.

His sceptre shows the force of *temporal* power,

h. o.

The *attribute* to awe and majesty,

a. o.

Wherein doth sit the dread and *fear* of kings :

h. o.

But mercy is *above* his sceptred sway,

a. o.

It is enthroned in the *hearts* of kings :

h. o.

It is an attribute to *God* Himself ;

a. f.

And *earthly* power doth then show likest *God's,*

h. o.   a. o.

When mercy seasons *justice.*

h. o.

9

CXXXVI.

Of *God* she sung, and of the mild
a. f.
Attendant *Mercy*, that beside
a. o.
His awful throne forever *smiled*.
a. l.

CXXXVII.

Now *fades the glimmering landscape on the sight*,
b. h. h. l. p.
And all the air a solemn *stillness* holds,
b. h. upl. a. o.
Save where the *beetle* wheels his droning flight,
h. l. ind.
And drowsy *tinklings lull* the distant folds.
h. o. b. ind. d. o. b. p.

CXXXVIII.

The strife of *fiends* is on the battling clouds,
b. h. a. o.
The *glare of hell* is in *these sulphurous lightnings;*
b. h. d. o.   b. h. a. o.
This is no *earthly* storm.
r. h. upl. a. o.   d. l.

CXXXIX.

United we *stand;* divided we *fall*.
b. h. h. f.   b. h. d. o.

CXL.

Time! *Time!* in thy triumphal flight
b. h. a. f.
How all life's phantoms *fleet away!*
b. h. h. l.

CXLI.

Ye different sects who *all* declare,
b. h. h. o.
Lo Christ is *here* and Christ is *there;*
h. f.   h. l.
Your *stronger* proofs divinely give,
d. o.
And tell me *where* the Christians *live*.
h. o.   imp.

CXLII.

His heart is far from *fraud*, as *heaven and earth*.

    h. l.   b. h. h. l.

CXLIII.

If you were *men*, as men you are in *show*,

    h. o.   h. l.

You would not *use* a gentle lady so.

        d. o.

CXLIV.

Time *past*, and time to *come are not*—

  h. l.   h. f.   d. l.

Time *present* is our lot.

    d. f.

CXLV.

Press bravely *onward!* — *not in vain*

    h. f.   h. l.

  Your generous *trust in human kind;*

            b. h. h. o.

The good which *bloodshed* could not gain,

        d. l.

  Your peaceful *zeal* shall find.

        b. h. d. o.

SELECTIONS FOR PRACTICE.

The following selections, as well as the preceding miscellaneous examples, have been chosen with special reference to the system presented in this work. In order more fully to illustrate the principles of the science, the notation, for the most part, exhibits the action in its full effect. It is by no means to be inferred, however, that so many gestures as are here indicated are absolutely necessary. Indeed, unless the words are spoken with sufficient deliberation to give ample time for the requisite transitions, and attended with the proper accompaniments of attitude, facial expression and tones of voice, this notation cannot be followed with good effect.

THE BATTLE OF WATERLOO.

BYRON.

There was a sound of revelry by *night*,
h. l. ind.
And Belgium's capital had gathered then

Her beauty and her *chivalry;* and bright
b. h. h. o.
The lamps shone o'er fair women and *brave* men.
b. h. h. l.

A *thousand hearts* beat *happily*, and when
 b. h. h. l.   imp.
Music arose with its voluptuous *swell*,
                              b. h. a. o.
Soft eyes looked *love* to eyes which spake *again ;*
              b. h. h. o.   imp.
And all went merry as a *marriage bell :*
                        b. h. a. o.
But *hush ! hark !* a deep sound strikes like a rising *knell !*
 h. o. p. h. f. ind.   a. l. ind.

Did ye not *hear* it ?   No, 't was but the *wind,*
           h. f.   a. l.
Or the *car* rattling o'er the stony street ;
       h. l.
On with the dance !   Let joy be *unconfined ;*
b. h. h. f.   b. h. h. l.
No sleep till *morn,* when Youth and *Pleasure* meet,
              a. l.   b. h. h. o.
To chase the glowing hours with flying *feet—*
                                     b. h. d. o.
But HARK ! — that heavy sound breaks in once *more,*
 h. f. ind.   h. l. ind.
As if the *clouds* its echo would *repeat ;*
          b. h. a. o.   imp.
And *nearer, clearer, deadlier* than before !
    b. h. d. f.   rep.   rep.
Arm ! ARM ! it *is* — it *is* — the *cannon's opening roar !*
 b. h. h. o.   h. f.   rep.   h. l. ind.

Ah ! then and there was *hurrying to and fro,*
                        b. h. h. o.
And gathering *tears,* and tremblings of *distress,*
              b. h. d. o.   b. h. d. l.
And cheeks all *pale,* which, but an hour ago,
               b. h. h. o. p.
Blushed at the praise of their own loveliness ;
b. h. d. o.
And there were sudden *partings,* such as press
                      b. h. d. l.
The *life* from out young hearts, and choking sighs
    b. h d. f.

Which *ne'er* might be repeated ; *who* could guess

b. h. upl.   drop.   h. o.

If ever more should *meet* those mutual eyes,

       b. h. h. f. .

Since upon night so *sweet*, such *awful morn* could rise?

       h. o.   b. h. upl.   drop.

And there was *mounting in hot haste ;* the *steed,*

      b. h. h. f.   imp.

The mustering *squadron*, and the clattering *car*,

     b. h. h. o.   b. h. h. f.

Went pouring *forward* with impetuous *speed,*

     rep.   rep.

And swiftly *forming* in the ranks of war :

     b. h. h. o.

And the deep *thunder*, peal on peal *afar ;*

    b. h. a. f.   b. h. h. l. par.

And *near*, the beat of the alarming *drum*

  h. f.   d. f.

Roused up the *soldier*, ere the morning *star ;*

    h. l.   a. l.

While *thronged* the citizens with terror *dumb*,

  b. h. h. o.   b. h. d. o.

Or whispering with white lips — " The *foe*, They COME !

           b. h. h. l. par.

They COME !"

  rep.

And Ardennes waves above them her *green leaves,*

            b. h. a. o.

Dewy, with nature's *tear-drops*, — as they pass,

        b. h. d. o. p.

Grieving — if aught inanimate e'er grieves —

b. h. upl. a. o.   drop.

Over the unreturning *brave* — alas !

       b. h. d. o. p.

Ere evening to be *trodden* like the *grass*

      b. h. d. o. p.   imp.

Which now *beneath* them, but *above* shall grow

    rep.   b. h. upl. h. o.

In its next verdure, when this fiery mass

drop.

Of *living* valor, *rolling* on the foe,

b. h. d. f.   rep.

And *burning* with high *hope*, shall moulder cold and *low*.

rep.   b. h. a. o.   drop.   b.h.d.o.p.

Last *noon* beheld them full of lusty *life*,

b. h. h. f.   imp.

Last eve in *Beauty's* circle proudly *gay*,

b. h. h. o.   b. h. h. l.

The midnight brought the signal sound of *strife*,

a. o. ind.

The morn, the marshalling in *arms*, — the day

b. h. h. o.

Battle's magnificently stern array !

b. h. h. f.

The thunder clouds closed *o'er* it, which when *rent*,

b. h. h. o. p.   b. h. h. l. p.

The earth is covered *thick* with *other* clay,

b. h. d. o. p.   imp.

Which her OWN clay shall cover, *heaped* and *pent*,

b. h. d. f. p.   b. h. a. o. par.   b. h. d. f. p.

Rider and *horse* — friend, *foe* — in one red burial *blent*.

rep.   b. h. d. o. p.   b.h.d.f.p.

THE LAUNCHING OF THE SHIP.

LONGFELLOW.

All is *finished*, and at length

d. o.

Has come the *bridal* day

b. h. h. o.

Of beauty and of *strength*.

b. h. d. o.

To-day the vessel shall be *launched!*

b. h. h. f.

With fleecy *clouds* the sky is blanched.

b. h. a. o.

And o'er the *bay*,

h. f.

Slowly, in all its *splendors* dight,
    b. h. h. o.

The great *sun* rises to *behold* the sight.
    b. h. h. f.   b. h. h. o.

The ocean old,
    b. h. h. o.

Centuries old,
    b. h. d. o.

Strong as *youth*, and as *uncontrolled*,
        h. l.   d. l.

Paces restless to and fro,
b. h. h. f.

Up and down the sands of *gold*.
                    b. h. d. f.

His beating heart is not at *rest*.
                    d. l.

And *far and wide*,
    b. h. h. l.

With ceaseless flow,
His beard of *snow*,
    b. h. d. o.

Heaves with the heaving of his *breast*.
b. h. h. o.   b. h. d. o.

He waits impatient for his *bride*.
                    b. h. h. f.

There she stands,
h. o. ind.

With her foot upon the *sands*,
                d. o.

Decked with flags and streamers *gay*,
                        a. l.

In honor of her *marriage-day*,
            b. h. a. o.

Her snow-white *signals*, *fluttering*, *blending*,
            a. o. ind.   a. l.   b. h h. f.

Round her like a *veil* descending,
            b.h.d,o.

Ready to be
b. h. h. f.

The bride of the *gray old sea*.
                b. h. h. l.

Then the *Master*,
h. o. ind.

With a gesture of command,

Waved his hand;
a. l.

And at the *word*,
h. o. ind.

Loud and sudden, there was heard,
b. h. upl.

All around them and *below*,
b. h. h. l.   b. h. d. o.

The sound of *hammers*, blow on *blow*,
d. o. cli.   rep.

Knocking away the shores and spurs.
d. l. p.

And *see!* she *stirs!*
h. f. ind.   h. f.

She *starts* — she *moves* — she seems to feel
b. h. h. f.   rep.

The thrill of *life* along her keel,
b. h. d. f.

And, *spurning with her foot* the ground,
d. l. p.

With one exulting, joyous *bound*,
b. h. h. f.

She *leaps* into the ocean's arms.
b. h. d. f.

And lo! from the assembled crowd

There rose a *shout*, prolonged and *loud*,
a. l.   rep.

That to the *ocean* seemed to say,
h. f.

" *Take* her, O bridegroom, old and gray;
b. h. h. f.

Take her to thy protecting arms,
rep.

With all her youth and all her *charms*."
b. h. h. o.

9*

How *beautiful* she is ! how *fair*

b. h. h. o.   b.h.h,f.

She lies within those arms, that press

Her form with many a soft *caress*

b. h. d. f.

Of tenderness and watchful *care !*

rep.

Sail *forth* into the sea, O ship !

b. h. h. f.

Through wind and *wave* right *onward* steer !

b.h.h.f.   rep.

The moistened *eye*, the trembling *lip*,

h. o.   h. l.

Are *not* the signs of doubt or fear.

d. l.

Sail forth into the *sea of life*,

b. h. h. o.

O gentle, loving, *trusting* wife,

b. h. d. f.

And safe from all *adversity*,

h. l.

Upon the *bosom* of that sea

b. h. h. o.

Thy comings and thy *goings* be !

b. h. h. l.

For gentleness, and love, and *trust*,

b. h. h. o.

Prevail o'er angry wave and *gust ;*

b. h. h. l.

And in the wreck of *noble lives*,

b. h. a. o.

Something *immortal* still survives !

b. h. a. f.

Thou *too* sail on, O Ship of State !

h. f.

Sail on, O *Union*, strong and great !

b. h. h. f.   rep.

Humanity, with all its *fears*,
b. h. h. o.   b. h. d. o.
With all the hopes of future *years*,
b. h. a. o.
Is hanging *breathless* on thy fate !
b. h. h. f.
We know what *Master* laid thy keel,
h. o.
What workmen wrought thy ribs of *steel*,
b. h. h. o.
Who made each mast and sail and *rope*,
h. o. ind.
What anvils rang, what *hammers* beat,
h. l.
In what a forge, and what a heat

Were shaped the anchors of thy *hope*.
d. o.

Fear not each sudden sound and shock ;
b. h. h. f.
'T is of the *wave*, and *not the rock ;*
d. o.   h. l. ind.
'T is but the flapping of the *sail*,
a. l.
And *not* a rent made by the gale.
h. o. b.
In spite of rock and tempest *roar*,
a. l.
In spite of false lights on the *shore*,
h. l.
Sail on, nor *fear* to breast the sea.
h. f.   rep.
Our *hearts*, our *hopes* are all with *thee :*
b. h. h. f.   b. h. a. f.   b. h. h. o.
Our *hearts*, our *hopes*, our *prayers*, our *tears*,
b. h. h. o.   b. h. a. o.   b. h. a. f.   b. h. d. o.
Our *faith* triumphant o'er our *fears*,
a. f.   a. l.
Are all with *thee* — are *all* with thee.
b. h. h. f.   b.h.h.o.

MARCO BOZZARIS.

HALLECK.

At midnight, in his guarded *tent,*

　　　　　　　　　h. l. ind.

　The *Turk* was dreaming of the hour,

　　rep.

When *Greece,* her knee in *suppliance* bent,

　　h. o.　　　　　　　　d. o.

　Should *tremble* at his power :

　　rep.

In *dreams,* through camp and court, he bore

　　h. o.

The trophies of a *conqueror ;*

　　　　　　a. o.

　In dreams his song of *triumph* heard ;

　　　　　　　　　a. l.

Then wore his monarch's signet *ring :*

　　　　　　　　　h. o. ind.

Then pressed that monarch's *throne* — a *king ;*

　　　　　　　　h. o.　　a. o.

As wild his thoughts, and gay of *wing,*

　　　　　　　　　a. l.

　As *Eden's* garden bird.

　a. o. b. ind.

At midnight, in the forest *shades,*

　　　　　　　　h. l.

　Bozzaris ranged his Suliote band

　h. l. ind.

True as the steel of their tried *blades,*

h. f.　　　　　　　　　rep.

　Heroes in heart and *hand.*

　a. o.　　　　　　d. o.

There had the Persian's *thousands* stood,

　　　　　　　　b. h. h. o.

There had the glad earth drunk their *blood,*

　　　　　　　　　　b. h. d. f.

　On old *Platea's* day :

　h. o. b.

And now there breathed that haunted air

The sons of sires who *conquered* there,
b. h. a. o.
With arms to *strike*, and souls to *dare*,
h. o. cli.   a. o. cli.
As *quick*, as *far* as they.
d. o. cli.   a. o. cli.

An hour pass'd on: the Turk *awoke;*
b. h. upl. a. o.
That bright dream was his last ;
drop.
He woke — to hear his *sentries* shriek,
h. l. ind.
" To *arms!* they *come!* the Greek ! the *Greek!* "
b. h. h. f.   b. h. h. l. par.   rep.
He woke — to *die* midst flame and *smoke,*
d. o.   b. h. a. o.
And shout, and groan, and *sabre*-stroke,
h. l. ind.
And *death*-shots falling thick and fast
b. h. a. o.
As *lightnings* from the mountain cloud ;
b. h. a. f.
And heard, with voice as *trumpet* loud,
a. l. ind.
    Bozzaris cheer his band :
h. l. ind.
" *Strike !* till the last arm'd foe *expires ;*
h. f. cli.   d. f. cli.
Strike ! for your altars and your *fires ;*
h. f. cli.   d. o. cli.
Strike ! for the green graves of your *sires ;*
h. f. cli.   h. l. cli.
    God, and your native *land!* "
h. l.

They fought like *brave* men, long and *well ;*
h. o.   d. o.
They *piled* that ground with Moslem slain ;
d. l. p.
They *conquer'd ;* but Bozzaris *fell,*
a o.   d. o. p.

Bleeding at every *vein.*
b. h. d. o.

His few surviving *comrades* saw
h. o.

His smile, when rang their proud *hurrah!*
a. l.

And the red field was *won;*
h. l.

Then saw in *death* his eyelids close,
d. o. p.

Calmly, as to a night's *repose,*
d. l. p.

Like flowers at set of *sun.*
rep.

Come to the bridal *chamber,* death!
b. h. h. l. par.

Come to the *mother,* when she feels,
h. l.

For the first time, her first-born's *breath;*
rep.

Come when the blessed seals

That close the *pestilence* are broke,
b. h. d. o.

And crowded *cities* wail its stroke;
b. h. h. l.

Come in *consumption's* ghastly form,
h. l. ind.

The *earthquake* shock, the *ocean* storm;
b. h. d. o.   b. h. h. o.

Come when the heart beats high and warm,

With banquet-song, and dance, and *wine,*
h. l.

And thou art *terrible!* the tear,
a. o. v.

The groan, the knell, the pall, the *bier;*
h. l. p.

And all we know, or dream, or *fear,*
b. h. a. o. v.

Of agony, are *thine.*
b. h. a. f.

But, to the *hero*, when his sword
a. l.
Has won the battle for the *free*,
b. h. h. l.
Thy voice sounds like a *prophet's* word,
a. o.
And in its hollow tones are heard

The thanks of *millions* yet to be.
b. h. a. o.
Bozzaris! with the storied brave,
d. f.
Greece nurtured, in her *glory's time*,
a. o.
Rest thee : there 's no *prouder* grave,
b. h. d. o.   a. o.
Even in her own proud *clime*.
a. l.
We tell thy doom without a *sigh;*
h. l.
For thou art *Freedom's* now, and *Fame's* —
a. o.   a. l.
One of the *few*, the *immortal names*,
h. f.   a. o.
That were not born to *die*.
d. o.

SPARTACUS TO THE GLADIATORS.

KELLOGG.

It had been a day of triumph in Capua. Lentulus, returning with victorious eagles, had amused the populace with the sports of the amphitheatre, to an extent hitherto unknown even in that luxurious *city*. The
h. l.
shouts of revelry had *died away;* the roar of the *lion*
d. l.   d. l. ind.

had ceased; the last loiterer had retired from the
drop.

banquet, and the lights in the palace of the *victor* were
l. h. h. l.   l. h. a. o. b.

extinguished.   The *moon*, *piercing* the tissue of fleecy
l. h. d. o. b.   a. f. ind.   rep.

clouds, *silvered* the dew-drop on the corselet of the
h. l.

Roman sentinel, and *tipped* the dark waters of Vol-
d. o. p.

turnus with *wavy*, tremulous light.   It was a night of
d. l. p.

holy calm, when the zephyr sways the young *spring*
h. l.

leaves, and whispers among the *hollow reeds* its dreamy
d l.

music.   No sound *was heard* but the last sob of some
h. l. p.

weary *wave*, telling the story to the pebbles of the
drop.

beach, and then all was *still* as the breast when the
d. l.   h. o. p.

spirit has departed.
drop.

In the deep recesses of the *amphitheatre*, a band of
b. h. h. o.

gladiators were crowded together — their muscles still
b. h. h. f.

knotted with the agony of *conflict*, the *foam* upon their
d. o. cli.   h. f. ind.

lips, and the scowl of *battle* yet lingering upon their
b. h. h. f.

brows — when *Spartacus*, rising in the midst of that
h. o.

grim assemblage, thus *addressed* them :
rep.

" Ye call me *chief;* and ye *do well* to call him chief,
h. o.   d. o.

who for twelve long years has met upon the arena

every shape of man or *beast* the broad empire of *Rome*
d. f.   h. l.

could furnish, and who never *yet* lowered his arm.   If
_{d. o.}

there be one *among* you who can say, that ever in public
_{h. o.}

fight or private *brawl*, my actions did belie my *tongue*, let
_{d. o.}   _{h. o.}

him stand forth, and *say* it.   If there be *three* in all your
_{h. f.}   _{h. o.}

company dare *face* me on the bloody sands, let them
_{h. o.}   _{h. f.}

come on.   And yet I was not always thus — a hired
_{b. h. h. f.}

butcher, a savage chief of still *more* savage men !
_{d. l.}   _{h. l.}

   " My ancestors came from old *Sparta*, and settled
_{h. o. b.}

among the vine-clad rocks and citron groves of *Cyra-*
_{h. l.}

cella.   My early *life* ran quiet as the brooks by which I
_{h. o.}

sported ; and when, at noon, I gathered the sheep be-
_{d. l.}

neath the *shade*, and played upon the shepherd's *flute*,
_{h. l.}   _{rep.}

there was a *friend*, the son of a *neighbor*, to *join* me in
_{h. o.}   _{rep.}   _{d. o.}

the pastime.   We led our flocks to the same *pasture*,
_{h. l.}

and partook together our rustic *meal*.
_{d. o.}

   " One evening, after the sheep were folded, and we

were all *seated* beneath the myrtle which shaded our
_{b. h. d. o.}

cottage, my *grandsire*, an old man, was telling of Mara-
_{h. o.}

thon, and *Leuctra ;* and how, in *ancient* times, a little
_{h. l.}   _{h. o. b.}

band of *Spartans*, in a defile of the mountains, had
_{h. l.}

withstood a *whole army*.   I did not then know what
_{b. h. h. l.}

war *was;* but my cheeks *burned;* I knew not *why,* and
d. o. rep. d. l.

I clasped the *knees* of that venerable man, until my
b. h. d. f.

mother, parting the hair from off my *forehead, kissed*
h. o. h. l. p. h. o.

my throbbing temples, and bade me go to *rest,* and
d. l.

think no more of those old tales and savage wars.

That very *night,* the *Romans* landed on our coast. I
h. o. ind. h. l.

saw the breast that had *nourished* me *trampled* by the
h. o. d. o. p.

hoof of the war-horse; the bleeding body of my *father*
h. o.

flung amid the blazing rafters of our *dwelling!*
a. l.

"To-day I *killed* a man in the arena; and when I
d. o.

broke his *helmet-clasps, behold!* he was my *friend.* He
h. o. r. h. a. o. upl. d. o.

knew me, smiled faintly, gasped, and *died* — the same
d. o.

sweet *smile* upon his lips that I had marked, when, in
h. o.

adventurous *boyhood,* we scaled the lofty *cliff* to pluck
h. l. a. l.

the first ripe *grapes,* and bear them *home* in childish
rep. h. l.

triumph! I told the prætor that the dead man had

been my *friend,* generous and *brave;* and I begged
h. o. d. o.

that I might *bear away* the body, to burn it on a *funeral*
h. l. a. l.

pile, and mourn over its ashes. Ay! upon my *knees,*
b. h. d. f.

amid the dust and blood of the arena, I *begged* that
rep.

poor boon, while all the assembled maids and *matrons,*
b. h. h. o.

and the holy virgins they call *Vestals*, and the *rabble*,

rep.   b. h. d. o.

shouted in *derision* deeming it rare *sport*, forsooth, to

b. h. h. l.   h. l.

see Rome's fiercest *gladiator* turn pale and *tremble* at

h. o. ind.   d. o. ind.

the sight of that piece of bleeding clay! And the

prætor *drew back* as I were *pollution*, and sternly said,

h. l.   d. l.

'Let the carrion *rot;* there are no *noble* men but

d. o. b.   h. o.

Romans!' And so, *fellow-gladiators*, must *you*, and so

d o.   b. h. h. o.   rep.

must *I*, die like *dogs*.

h. f.   d. l.

"O, Rome! *Rome!* thou hast been a tender *nurse* to

b. h. h. o.   d. o.

me! Ay! thou hast given, to that poor, gentle, timid

shepherd lad, who never knew a harsher tone than a

flute-note, *muscles* of iron and a heart of *flint;* taught

h. l.   b. h. d. f. cli.   r. h. on heart, cli.

him to drive the sword through plaited mail and links

of rugged *brass*, and warm it in the marrow of his *foe;*

b. h. d. o. cli.   d. o. cli.

to gaze into the glaring eye-balls of the fierce Numidian

lion, even as a boy upon a laughing *girl!* And he shall

h. f.   h. l.

pay thee *back*, until the yellow Tiber is red as frothing

d. f. cli.

wine, and in its deepest ooze thy *life-blood* lies curdled!

rep.   rep.

"Ye stand here, now, like *giants*, as ye are! The

b. h. h. o.

strength of *brass*-toughened sinews; but *to-morrow*,

d. o. cli.   h. o.

some Roman *Adonis*, breathing sweet perfume from his

h. l.

curly locks, shall, with his lily fingers, *pat* your red
d. l.　　　　　　　　　　　　　　　　　　　　h. o. p.

brawn, and bet his *sestérces* upon your blood.　*Hark!*
　　　　　　　　d. l.　　　　　　　　　　　　　　h. l. ind.

hear ye you *lion* roaring in his den?　'T is *three days*
　　　　rep.　　　　　　　　　　　　　　　　　　d. o.

since he tasted flesh; but *to-morrow* he shall break his
　　　　　　　　　　　　　　h. o.

fast upon *yours*—and a *dainty meal* for him ye will be!
d. o.　　　　　　　　　d. l.

　　" If ye are *beasts*, then *stand* here like fat oxen, wait-
　　　　　　　d. o.　　　　h. o.

ing for the *butcher's* knife!　If ye are *men*, follow *me!*
　　　　　h. l. ind.　　　　　　　　　　h. f.　　　　h. o.

Strike down yon guard, gain the *mountain passes*, and
h. l ind.　　　　　　　　　　　　　　a. l.

there do *bloody* work, as did your sires at old *Ther-*
　　　　d. o. cli.　　　　　　　　　　　　　　　h. l.

mopylæ! Is Sparta *dead?*　Is the old Grecian spirit *frozen*
　　　　　　　　h. o.　　　　　　　　　　　　　　d. o.

in your veins, that ye do crouch and cower like a

belabored *hound* beneath his master's lash?　O, com-
　　　　h. l. ind.

rades! *warriors! Thracians!*—if we *must* fight, let us
　　b. h. h. o.　　　b. h. h. l.　　　　　b. h. h. o.

fight for *ourselves!* If we *must* slaughter, let us
　　b. h. d. o.　　　　　　b. h. h. o.

slaughter our *oppressors!* If we *must* die, let it be
　　　　　b. h. d. o.　　　　　　rep.

under a *clear sky*, by the bright *waters*, in *noble*,
　　b. h. a. o.　　　　　　　　b. h. d. o.　　　b. h. h. o.

honorable *battle!*"
　　rep.

PARRHASIUS.

WILLIS.

Parrhasius stood, gazing forgetfully

Upon his canvass.　*There* Prometheus lay,
　　　　　　　h. f. ind.

Chained to the cold rocks of Mount Caucasus,

The *vultures* at his vitals, and the links

<small>h. f. v.</small>
Of the lame Lemnian *festering* in his flesh;

<small>h. l. p.</small>
And, as the painter's mind felt through the dim,

Rapt *mystery*, and plucked the shadows wild

<small>h. o. p.</small>
Forth with his reaching *fancy*, and with form

<small>a. o.</small>
And color *clad* them, his fine, earnest *eye*,

<small>h. f. p.   h. o. ind.</small>
Flashed with a passionate *fire*, and the quick curl

<small>a. o. ind.   rep.</small>
Of his thin nostril, and his quivering lip,

Were like the winged *god's*, breathing from his flight.

<small>a. o. ind.</small>

"Bring me the *captive* now!

<small>h. l. ind.</small>
My hand feels *skillful*, and the shadows *lift*

<small>h. o.   r. h. upl.</small>
From my waked spirit airily and *swift;*

<small>a. o. v.</small>

And I could paint the bow

Upon the bended *heavens;* around me play

<small>a. o.</small>
Colors of such *divinity* to-day.

<small>a. l.</small>

"*Ha!* bind him on his *back!*

<small>r. h. upl.   d. o. p.</small>
Look! as Prometheus in my *picture* here!

<small>h. f. ind.   rep.</small>
Quick! or he *faints!* stand with the *cordial* near!

<small>r. h upl.   d. o. ind.   h. l. ind.</small>
Now, bend him to the *rack!*

<small>d. f. ind.</small>

Press down the prisoned links into his flesh !
d. f. p.
And *tear agape* that healing wound afresh !
d. l.

" *So!* let him writhe !   How long
d. l. p.
Will he *live* thus ?   *Quick*, my good pencil, now !
d. f.   h. f. ind.
What a fine *agony* works upon his brow !
d. o.

Ha! grey-haired, and so strong !
r. h. upl.
How fearfully he *stifles* that short moan !
d. o. p.
Gods! if I could but *paint* a dying groan !
r. h. upl. a. o.   h. f.

" ' *Pity* ' thee ? so I *do ;*
d. o.   rep.
I pity the dumb victim at the *altar ;*
h. l. ind.
But does the robed *priest* for his pity falter ?
h. l.
I 'd *rack* thee, though I knew
d. o. ind.
A *thousand* lives were perishing in thine ;
d. o. cli.
What were *ten thousand* to a fame like mine ?
d. l.

" Ah ! there 's a deathless *name !*
a. o.
A spirit that the smothering vault shall *spurn,*
d. l. ind.
And, like a steadfast planet, mount and *burn ;*
a. o. ind.

And though its crown of flame

Consumed my brain to *ashes* as it won me ;
d. o. p.
By all the fiery *stars !* I 'd pluck it *on* me !
b. h. upl.   b. h. h. f. cli.

" Ay, though it bid me rifle

My *heart's last fount* for its insatiate thirst;
r. h. on heart, cli.
Though every life-strung nerve be *maddened* first;
b. h. d. f. cli.
Though it should bid me stifle

The yearning in my *throat* for my sweet child,
r. h. on throat, cli.
And *taunt* its mother till my brain went *wild!*
d. l.   d. o. cli.

" All! I would do it *all,*
b. h. d. o. cli.
Sooner than die like a *dull worm,* to *rot;*
d. l. ind.   rep.
Thrust foully in the *earth* to be *forgot,*
d. o. p.   d. l. p.
Oh *heavens!* but I appall
r. h. upl.
Your *heart,* old man! *forgive* — *ha!* on your *lives*
d. f.   rep.   r. h. upl.   d. o.
Let him not faint! *rack* him till he revives!
d. o.

" *Vain* — *vain* — *give o'er.* His *eye*
r. h. upl.   d. l. p.   d. o. b. p.   d. o. ind.
Glazes apace. He does not *feel* you now.
drop.
Stand *back!* I 'll paint the death dew on his *brow!*
d. l. p.   d. o. ind.
Gods! if he do not die
r. h. upl. a. o.
But for one *moment* — *one* — till I eclipse
d. o. ind.   rep.
Conception with the scorn of those calm *lips!*
a. o.   d. o.

" *Shivering!* *Hark!* he *mutters*
r. h. upl. a. o.   a. l. ind.   d. o. ind.
Brokenly now; *that* was a difficult breath;
d. o. ind.

Another?　Wilt thou *never* come, oh, Death?
r. h. upl.　　　　　　　　　　d. o.

　　Look! how his temple flutters!
　　d. o. ind.

Is his heart *still?*　*Aha!* lift up his *head!*
　　　　　d. o.　r. h. upl.　　　　　d. o.

He *shudders*—*gasps*—*Jove* help him—so he 's dead!"
　d. o. p.　　　r. h. upl.　rep., but higher.　　　drop.

How like a mounting *devil* in the heart
　　　　　　　　d. f.

Rules this unreined *ambition!*　Let it once
　　　　　　　　d. o.

But play the *monarch*, and its haughty brow
　　　　　h. o.

Glows with a beauty that bewilders *thought*
　　　　　　　　　　　　h o. p.

And unthrones peace *forever*.　Putting on
　　　　　　　　d. l.

The very pomp of *Lucifer*, it turns
　　　　　　　a. o.

The heart to *ashes*, and with not a spring
　　　　　d. o.

Left in the desert for the spirit's *lip*,
d. l.　　　　　　　　　　　h. o.

We look upon our *splendor*, and forget
　　　　　　　a. o.

The thirst of which we *perish!*
　　　　　　　　d. o.

THE BURIAL OF SIR JOHN MOORE.

WOLFE.

Not a *drum* was heard, not a funeral *note*,
　h. o. ind.　　　　　　　　　d. o. ind.

　As his corse to the *rampart* we hurried;
　　　　　　　h. l.

Not a *soldier* discharged his farewell shot
　d. o. ind.

　O'er the grave where our hero we buried.

We buried him *darkly* at dead of *night*,
    h. l.   imp.
  The sods with our *bayonets* turning;
             d. o.
By the struggling *moon-beam's* misty light,
             a. o.
  And the *lantern* dimly burning.
    d. l. ind

No useless *coffin* enclosed his breast,
        d. l.
  Nor in sheet nor in *shroud* we wound him;
             b. h. d. o.
But he lay like a warrior taking his *rest*,
                 d. f.
  With his martial *cloak* around him.
    b. h. d. f.

Few and short were the *prayers* we said;
              h. l.
  And we spake not a word of *sorrow;*
              d. l.
But we steadfastly *gazed* on the face of the dead,
      b. h. d. f.
  As we bitterly thought of the *morrow*.
              h. f.

We thought, as we hollowed his narrow *bed*,
                 b. h. d. f.
  And *smoothed* down his lonely pillow,
  b. h. d. o. p.
That the *foe* and the *stranger* would tread o'er his head,
    h. o.   h. l.
  And we *far away* on the billow.
    h. o. b.

Lightly they 'll talk of the spirit that 's gone,
h. l.
  And o'er his cold *ashes* upbraid him;
          d. o.
  10

But little *he 'll reck*, if they let him sleep on
    d. l.
  In the grave where a *Briton* has laid him.
        d. o.

But *half* of our heavy task was done,
    d. o.
  When the *clock* struck the hour for retiring ;
        a. l.
And we heard the distant and random *gun*
            h. l. ind.
  ·That the *foe* was sullenly firing.
        imp.

Slowly and sadly we *laid him down*,
        b. h. d. f.
  From the field of his fame fresh and *gory :*
            rep.
We carved not a *line*, we raised not a *stone*,
        d. o. ind.   h. o. ind.
  But we left him *alone* in his glory.
        d. o.

HOHENLINDEN.

CAMPBELL.

On *Linden*, when the sun was *low*,
    h. o. ind.   h. l. ind.
All bloodless lay the untrodden *snow ;*
                d. l. p.
And dark as winter was the flow

Of *Iser*, rolling rapidly.
    d. l.

But Linden saw *another* sight,
        h. o.
When the drum *beat* at dead of night,
            h. l. ind.

Commanding fires of *death*, to *light*
b. h. d. f.   b. h. a. o.
The darkness of her scenery.

By torch and trumpet fast *arrayed*,
b. h. h. o.
Each horseman drew his battle *blade*,
h. o. ind.
And *furious* every charger neighed
b. h. h. o.
To *join* the dreadful revelry.
b. h. h. f,

Then shook the hills with *thunder* riven,
b. h. a. o.
Then rushed the *steed* to battle driven,
b. h. h. f.
And louder than the bolts of *Heaven*,
b. h. a. o.
Far flashed the red artillery.
b. h. a. l.

And redder *yet* those fires shall glow,
h. o.
On Linden's hills of blood-stained snow;

And darker *yet* shall be the flow
d. o. p.
Of *Iser* rolling rapidly.
d. l.

'T is morn, but scarce yon lurid *sun*
h. f. ind.
Can *pierce* the war-clouds, rolling dun,
imp.
When furious Frank, and fiery *Hun*,
b. h. h. o.
Shout in their sulphurous canopy.
b. h a. o.

The combat *deepens*.   *On*, ye brave,

b. h. h. o.   b. h. h. f.

Who rush to *glory* or the *grave!*

b. h. a. o.   b. h. d. l.

Wave, Munich! *all* thy banners wave,

h l.   b. h. h. l.

And *charge* with all thy chivalry !

b. h. h. f.

Ah! few shall *part* where *many* meet!

h. o. p.   b. h. h. o.

The *snow* shall be their winding sheet,

b. h. d. o. p.

And every turf beneath their *feet*

b. h. d. o.

Shall be a soldier's *sepulchre*.

b. h. d. f.

CHARACTER OF NAPOLEON BONAPARTE.

CHANNING.

To bring together in a narrower compass what seem to us the great leading features of the intellectual and moral character of Napoleon Bonaparte, we may remark that his intellect was distinguished by rapidity of *thought*. He understood by a *glance* what most men,

h. o. ind.   h. o.

and superior men, could only learn by *study*. He

d. o.

darted to a conclusion rather by *intuition* than reason-

h. f. ind.   h. f.

ing. In war, which was the only subject of which he was *master*, he seized in an *instant* on the great'points

h. o.   h. f.

of his own and his enemy's positions; and *combined* at

b. h. h. f.

once the movements by which an overpowering force
might be thrown with unexpected *fury* on a vulnerable
b. h. d. f.
part of the hostile line, and the fate of an army be
decided in a *day*. He understood war as a *science;* but
d. o. h. o.
his mind was too *bold*, rapid, and *irrepressible*, to be
h. f. d. f.
enslaved by the technics of his profession. He found
d. o.
the old armies fighting by *rule;* and he discovered the
h. f.
true characteristic of *genius*, which, without *despising*
h. o. h. l.
rules, knows when and how to *break* them. He under-
d. o.
stood thoroughly the immense moral *power* which is
b. h. h. o.
gained by originality and *rapidity* of operation. He
b. h. d. o.
astonished and *paralysed* his enemies by his unforeseen
h. l. p.
and impetuous assaults, by the *suddenness* with which
b. h. h. o.
the storm of battle burst upon them; and, whilst giving
to his soldiers the advantages of *modern* discipline,
h. o.
breathed into them, by his quick and decisive movements, the enthusiasm of *ruder ages*. This power of
a. o. b.
disheartening the *foe*, and of spreading through his own
d. l.
ranks a confidence, and exhilarating *courage*, which
b. h. a. o.
made war a *pastime*, and seemed to make victory *sure*,
h. l. h. f.
distinguished Napoleon in an age of *uncommon* military
h. o.

talent, and was one main instrument of his **future**

power.
d. o.

The wonderful *effects* of that rapidity of thought by
h. f.
which Bonaparte was marked, the signal *success* of his
h. o.
new mode of warfare, and the almost incredible speed
with which his fame was spread through *nations*, had
h. l.
no small agency in *fixing* his character, and determining
h. f.
for a period the fate of *empires*. These stirring influ-
b. h. d. o.
ences infused a new consciousness of his own *might*.
d. o.
They gave intensity and audacity to his *ambition ;* gave
h. o.
form and substance to his indefinite visions of *glory*,
a. o.
and raised his fiery hopes of *empire*. The burst of
b. h. a. o.
admiration which his early career called forth, must, in
b. h. h. l.
particular, have had an influence in imparting to his
ambition that *modification* by which it was characterised,
b. h. d. o.
and which contributed alike to its *success* and to its *fall*.
h. o.   d. o.
He began with *astonishing* the world; with producing
b. h. h. l.
a sudden and universal *sensation*, such as modern times
rep.
had not *witnessed*. To *astonish*, as well as to *sway*, by
b. h. d. o.   h. o.   h. l. p.
his energies, became the great aim of his *life*. Hence-
d. o.
forth to rule was not *enough* for Bonaparte. He wanted
d. l.

to *amaze*, to *dazzle*, to *overpower* men's souls, by striking,
r. h. upl.   h. o. p.   b. h. d. l.

bold, magnificent, and *unanticipated* results.   To govern
b. h. h. f.   b. h. d. o.

ever so *absolutely* would not have *satisfied* him, if he
h. l.   d. o.

must have governed *silently*.   He wanted to reign
d. l.

through *wonder* and *awe*, by the grandeur and terror of
r. h. upl.   h. o. p.

his *name*, by displays of power which would rivet on
h. f.

him every *eye*, and make him the theme of every
b. h. h. f.

tongue.   *Power* was his supreme object; but a power
b. h. h. l.   h. o.

which should be *gazed* at as well as *felt*, which should
h. f.   h. o.

strike men as a *prodigy*, which should shake old thrones
d. o.

as an *earthquake*, and, by the suddenness of its new
b. h. d. o.

creations, should awaken something of the submissive

wonder which *miraculous* agency inspires.
r. h. upl.   a. o.

Such seems to us to have been the *distinction* or
h. o.

characteristic modification of his love of *fame*. It was
rep.

a diseased passion for a kind of admiration, which, from

the principles of our nature, cannot be *enduring*, and
h. l.

which demands for its support perpetual and more

stimulating *novelty*. Mere esteem he would have *scorned*.
d. o.   h. l. v.

Calm admiration, though universal and enduring, would

have been *insipid*.   He wanted to *electrify* and over-
d. o.   b. h. a. f.

whelm. He lived for *effect.* The world was his *theatre;*
b.h.d.o.p.   d. o.   h. l.

and he cared little what *part* he played, if he might
d. l.

walk the sole *hero* on the stage, and call forth bursts of
a. o.

applause which would *silence* all other fame. In war,
b. h. a. o.   b. h. d. o. p.

the triumphs which he coveted were those in which he

seemed to *sweep away his foes* like a whirlwind; and
b. h. h. l. v. par.

the immense and unparalleled *sacrifice* of his own
b. h. d. l.

soldiers, in the rapid marches and daring assaults to

which he owed his victories, in no degree *diminished*
d. o.

their worth to the victor. In peace, he delighted to

hurry through his dominions; to *multiply* himself by his
h. l.   b. h. h. o.

rapid movements; to gather at a *glance* the capacities
h. o. ind.

of improvement which every important place *possessed;*
b. h. d. o.

to suggest plans which would *startle* by their originality
r. h. upl.

and *vastness;* to project, in an *instant,* works which a
h. l.   h. f.

life could not accomplish, and to leave behind the
h. l.

impression of a *superhuman* energy.
d. o.

Our sketch of Bonaparte would be imperfect indeed,

if we did not add, that he was characterised by nothing

more strongly than by the spirit of *self-exaggeration.*
b. h. h. o.

The singular energy of his intellect and *will,* through
h. o.

which he had mastered so many rivals and *foes*, and
_{h. l.}
overcome what seemed *insuperable* obstacles, inspired a
_{b. h. h. f.}
a consciousness of being something *more* than man.
_{b. h. d. o.}
His strong original tendencies to pride and *self-exalta-*
_{h. o.}
tion, fed and pampered by strange success and *un-*
bounded applause, swelled into an almost insane con-
_{b. h. h. l.}
viction of *superhuman* greatness. In his own view, he
_{b. h. a. o.}
stood *apart* from other men. *He* was not to be measured
_{h. l.}   _{h. o.}
by the standard of humanity. *He* was not to be retarded
_{rep.}
by difficulties, to which all *others* yielded. *He* was not
_{h. l.}   _{h. o.}
to be subjected to laws and obligations which all others
were expected to obey. Nature and the human will
were to bend to *his* power. He was the child and
_{d. o.}
favorite of *fortune ;* and, if not the *lord*, the chief *object*
_{h. o.}   _{h. l.}   _{d. o.}
of destiny. His history shows a spirit of self-exaggeration *unrivalled* in enlightened ages, and which reminds
_{d. o.}
us of an Oriental *king* to whom incense had been burnt
_{h. o. b.}
from his *birth* as to a deity. This was the chief source
_{d. o.}
of his *crimes.* He wanted the sentiment of a common
_{d. f.}
nature with his *fellow-beings.* He had no *sympathies*
_{h. o.}   _{d. l.}
with his race. That feeling of *brotherhood*, which is
_{h. o.}

10*

developed in truly *great* souls with peculiar energy, and
_{rep.}

through which they give up themselves *willing* victims,
_{b. h. d. o.}

joyful *sacrifices*, to the interests of mankind, was wholly
_{rep.}

unknown to him.   *His* heart, amidst all its wild *beatings*,
_{b. h. d. l.}   _{h. o.}   _{rep.}

never had one *throb* of disinterested love.   The ties
_{h. l.}

which bind man to *man* he broke *asunder*.   The proper
_{b. h. h. f.}   _{b. h. d. l.}

happiness of a man, which consists in the victory of

moral energy and social affection over the selfish pas-
_{a. o.}

sions, *he cast away* for the lonely joy of a *despot*.   With
_{d. l.}   _{h. l. ind.}

powers which might have made him a glorious repre-

sentative and minister of the beneficent *Divinity*, and
_{a. o.}

with natural sensibilities which might have been exalted

into sublime *virtues*, he chose to *separate* himself from
_{b h a. o.}   _{h. l. v.}

his kind — to *forego* their love, esteem, and gratitude
_{d. l.}

— that he might become their *gaze*, their *fear*, their
_{h. f}   _{h. o. v.}

wonder ; and for this selfish, *solitary* good, parted with
_{h. l.}   _{h. f.}

peace and imperishable *renown*.
_{d. o.}

BERNARDO DEL CARPIO.

MRS. HEMANS.

The warrior *bowed* his crested head, and *tamed* his heart
of fire,   _{h. o. p.}   _{d. o. p.}

And sued the haughty *king* to free his long-imprisoned
sire ;   _{h. o.}

"I bring thee here my *fortress*-keys, I bring my captive
    train,
h. f.
h. o.

I pledge thee *faith*, my liege, my lord!—O! *break* my
    father's chain!"
d. f.
b. h. h. f. cla.

"*Rise*, rise! even *now* thy father comes, a *ransomed*
    man, this day!
r. h. upl.
d. f.
d. o.

Mount thy good *horse;* and thou and I will *meet* him
    on his way."
h. o.
h. f.

Then lightly rose that loyal son, and *bounded* on his
    steed,
h. o.

And *urged*, as if with lance in rest, the charger's foamy
    speed.
h. f.

And lo! from *far*, as *on* they pressed, there came a
    glittering band,
h. f. ind.
h. f.
h. o.

With one that 'midst them *stately* rode, as a *leader* in
    the land;
h. o.
a. o.

"Now *haste*, Bernardo, *haste!* for there, in very *truth*,
    is he,
h. f.
rep.
rep.

The *father* whom thy faithful heart hath yearned so
    long to see."
rep.
d. f.

His dark eye *flashed*, his proud breast *heaved*, his cheek's
    hue came and *went;*
h. o. ind.
h. o.
h. l.

He reached that gray-haired chieftain's *side*, and there,
    dismounting, *bent;*
h. o.
d. o.

A *lowly* knee to earth he bent, his father's hand he
d. o.
took —
h. o.
What *was* there in its touch that all his fiery spirit
d. o.
shook ?

That hand was *cold* — a *frozen* thing — it *dropped* from
h. o. p.   rep.   drop.
his like lead !
He looked up to the face above — the face was of the
dead !
A *plume* waved o'er the noble brow — the brow was
a. o.
fixed and white ;
r. h. upl.
He *met*, at last, his father's eyes — but in them was no
h. o.   drop.
sight !

Up from the ground he sprang and *gazed ;* but who
r. h. upl.   h. f.
could *paint* that gaze ?
d. o.
They hushed their very *hearts*, that saw its horror and
amaze —   h. o. p.
They might have *chained* him, as before that stony
form he stood ;   d. o.
For the power was *stricken* from his arm, and from his
lip the blood.   drop.

" *Father !* " at length he murmured low, and wept like
r. h. upl.
childhood then :
d. o.

Talk not of *grief* till thou hast seen the tears of *warlike*
    men ! _{h.l.}   _{d. o.}

He thought on all his glorious *hopes*, and all his young
    renown — _{a. o.}
    _{a. l.}

He flung his *falchion* from his side, and in the *dust* sat
    down.   _{d. l.}   _{d. o.}

Then covering with his steel-gloved hand his darkly
    mournful brow,

" No more, there is no more," he said, " to lift the sword
    for, now ;

My king is *false* — my hope *betrayed !* My father — O !
    _{d. o.}   _{d. l.}
    the *worth*,
    _{r. h. upl.}

The glory, and the loveliness are passed away from
    earth !   _{drop.}

" I thought to stand where *banners* waved, my sire,
    beside thee yet !   _{a. o.}

I would that there our kindred blood on Spain's *free*
    soil had met !   _{a. l.}

Thou wouldst have known my *spirit*, then — for *thee*
    my fields were won ;   _{h. o.}   _{rep.}

And thou hast perished in thy chains, as though thou
                    _{drop.}
    hadst no son ! "

Then, *starting* from the ground once more, he *seized* the
    _{r. h. upl.}   _{a. f. cli.}
    monarch's rein,

Amid the pale and wildered looks of all the courtier
    train ;

And, with a fierce, o'ermastering *grasp*, the rearing
    war-horse led,
rep.

And sternly set them face to *face* — the king before the
    dead :
b. h. h. f.
rep.

" Came I not forth, upon thy *pledge*, my father's hand
    to kiss ?
h. f.

Be *still*, and gaze thou *on*, false king ! and tell me what
h. f. p.   rep.
    is *this?*
d. o.

The voice, the glance, the *heart* I sought — give *answer*,
    where are they ?
h. o.
h. f.
d. o.

If thou wouldst clear thy *perjured* soul, send *life* through
    this cold clay ?
h. f. ind.
h. o.

" Into these glassy eyes put *light* — be *still!* keep *down*
    thine ire !
rep.
h. f. p.
rep.

Bid these white lips a *blessing* speak — this earth is *not*
    my sire —
h. o.
d. o.

Give me *back* him for whom I strove, for whom my
    blood was shed !
h. f.
d. f.

Thou *canst* not ? — and a *king !* — his dust be *mountains*
    on thy head !"
h. f.
d. f.
b. h. h. f. p.

He *loosed* the steed — his slack hand *fell* — upon the
h. o.   drop.
    silent face

He cast one long, deep, *troubled* look, then *turned* from
    that sad place ;
h. o. p.
rep., turning the body to left.

His hope was *crushed*, his after fate *untold* in martial
    strain —
d. o. p.
h. l.

His banner led the spears *no more*, amid the hills of
    Spain.
d. l.

THE INSPIRATION OF THE BIBLE.

EDW. WINTHROP.

Such is the intrinsic excellence of Christianity that it is adapted to the wants of *all*, and it *provides* for all,
<small>h. l.</small> <small>d. o.</small>
not only by its precepts and by its *doctrines*, but also
<small>h. l.</small>
by its *evidence*.
<small>d. o.</small>

The poor man may know nothing of history, or science, or *philosophy;* he may have read scarcely any
<small>h. l.</small>
book but the *Bible;* he may be totally unable to van-
<small>d. l.</small>
quish the skeptic in the arena of public *debate;* but he
<small>h. o.</small>
is nevertheless surrounded by a panoply which the shafts of infidelity can *never* pierce.
<small>d. o.</small>

You may go to the home of the poor *cottager*, whose
<small>h. l. ind.</small>
heart is deeply imbued with the spirit of vital *Christi-*
<small>d. o.</small>
anity; you may see him gather his little *family* around
<small>b. h. h. o.</small>
him: he expounds to them the wholesome doctrines and principles of the *Bible*, and if they want to know the
<small>h. o.</small>
evidence upon which he rests his faith of the divine
<small>d. o.</small>
origin of his religion, he can tell them, upon reading the book which teaches Christianity, he finds not only a perfectly true description of his own natural *character*,
<small>h. o.</small>

but in the provisions of this religion a perfect adaptation to all his *needs.*

It is a religion by which to *live* — a religion by which
h. l.
to *die;* a religion which *cheers* in darkness, *relieves* in
h. f.
perplexity, *supports* in adversity, keeps *steadfast* in
d. f.   h. f.   h. o.
prosperity, and guides the inquirer to that *blessed land*
h. l.   h. f.
where " the wicked *cease* from troubling, and the weary
a. o.
are at rest."
d. o.

We entreat you, therefore, to give the Bible a *wel-*
h. o.
come — a cordial *reception; obey* its precepts, *trust* its
rep.   d. o.   h. f.
promises, and rely implicitly upon that Divine *Redeemer,*
a. o.
whose religion brings glory to God in the *highest,* and
b. h. a. f.
on earth, *peace,* and good *will* to men.
b. h. h. o.   b. h. d. o.
Thus will you fulfill the noble end of your *existence,*
a. o.
and the *great God* of the universe will be your father
r. h. upl.
and your *friend;* and when the last mighty convulsion
h. o.
shall shake *the earth, and the sea,* and the sky, and the
b. h. h. l.
fragments of a *thousand barks,* richly freighted with
b. h. h. o.
intellect and *learning,* are scattered on the shores of
rep.
error and *delusion,* your vessel shall in safety *outride*
b. h. h. l. p.   b. h. a. o.
the storm, and enter in triumph the haven of eternal

rest.
b. h. a. f.

THE BRIDGE OF SIGHS.

HOOD.

One more unfortunate,

Weary of breath,

Rashly *importunate*,
        d. o.
Gone to her *death!*
        d. l.

Take her up *tenderly*,
        b. h. d. o. par.
Lift her with *care;*
        b. h. h. o. par.
Fashioned so *slenderly*,
        h. o.
Young, and so *fair!*
        d. o.

Look at her *garments*
        d. o. ind.
Clinging like cerements;

Whilst the wave constantly

Drips from her clothing;
d. o. p.
Take her up *instantly*,
        d. o.
Loving, not *loathing*,
imp.   d. l.
Touch her not *scornfully*,
        d. o.
Think of her *mournfully*,
        h. o. p.
Gently and *humanly;*
        d. o.
Not of the *stains* of her —
        d. l.

All that remains of her

Now is pure *womanly*.
h. o.

Make no deep *scrutiny*
h. o. p.
Into her mutiny

Rash and *undutiful;*
d. o.
Past all dishonor,
d. l.
Death has left on her

Only the *beautiful*.
h. o.

Loop up her *tresses*
d. o. ind.
Escaped from the comb,

Her fair auburn *tresses;*
d. o.
While *wonderment* guesses
r. h. upl.
Where was her *home?*
h. l.

Who was her *father?*
h. f.
Who was her *mother?*
h. o.
Had she a *sister?*
h. l.
Had she a *brother?*
d. o.
Or was there a *dearer* one
d. f.
Still, and a *nearer* one
rep.
Yet, than all other?

Alas! for the rarity
r. h. upl.
Of Christian *charity*
d. o.
Under the sun !

Oh ! it was *pitiful!*
h o. p.
Near a whole *city full*
b. h. h. o.
Home she had *none !*
d. l.

Sisterly, brotherly,

Fatherly, *motherly*
h. l.
Feelings had *changed :*
d. o.
Love by harsh evidence

Thrown from its *eminence :*
d. l.
Even God's *providence*
r. h. upl.
Seeming *estranged.*
h. l. p.

When the lamps quiver

So far in the *river,*
h. f. p.
With many a *light*
h. o.
From window and casement,

From garret to *basement,*
d. o.
She stood with *amazement,*
r. h. upl.
Houseless by night.
d. l.

The bleak wind of March

Made her *tremble and shiver;*

h. o. p.

But not the dark *arch,*

h. l.

Or the black flowing *river:*

d. f.

Mad from *life's* history,

h. o.

Glad to *death's* mystery

d. o.

Swift to be hurled —

Anywhere, anywhere,

h. l.

Out of the *world* —

d. l.

In she plunged *boldly,*

b. h. d. f.

No matter how coldly

d. l.

The rough river ran.

Take her up *tenderly,*

b. h. d. o. par.

Lift her with *care;*

b. h. h. o. par.

Fashioned so *slenderly,*

h. o.

Young, and so *fair!*

d. o.

Ere her limbs frigidly

Stiffen too *rigidly,*

d. o. p.

Decently, kindly,

Smooth, and *compose* them;

d. o. p.

And her *eyes, close* them,
  <small>d. o. 、 d. o. p.</small>
Staring so *blindly!*
  <small>d. o. p.</small>

Dreadfully staring
  <small>d. f.</small>
Through muddy *impurity*,
  <small>h. f. p.</small>
As when with the daring

Last look of *despairing*
  <small>r. h. upl.</small>
Fixed on *futurity*.
  <small>h. f.</small>

Perishing *gloomily*,
  <small>d. o. p.</small>
Spurred by *contumely*,
  <small>d. f.</small>
Cold *inhumanity*,
  <small>h. o. p.</small>
Burning *insanity*,
  <small>d. o. ind.</small>
Into her rest.—

Cross her hands *humbly*
  <small>d. o. p.</small>
As if praying dumbly,

Over her breast.

Owning her weakness,
  <small>d. o.</small>
Her evil *behavior*,
  <small>d. l.</small>
And leaving, with *meekness*,
  <small>d. o.</small>
Her sins to her Saviour!

THE BARON'S LAST BANQUET.

ALBERT G. GREENE.

O'er the low couch the setting sun had thrown his
latest *ray*,
d. o. p.
Where, in his last strong agony, a dying *warrior* lay,—
d. o.
The stern old *Baron Rudiger*, whose frame had ne'er
been *bent*   h. o.
d. o.
By wasting pain, till time and toil its iron strength had
spent.
d. l.

" They come *around* me here, and say my days of life
are *o'er*,   h. o.
d. o.
That I shall mount my noble *steed* and lead my band
no more;   h. o.
h. l.
They come, and, to my beard, they dare to tell me now
that *I*,
h. f.
Their own liege lord and *master* born, that I—*ha! ha!*
—must *die.*   h. o.   r. h. upl.
d. f.

" And what *is* death ?   I 've dared it *oft*, before the
h. o.   d. o.
    Paynim spear ;
Think ye he 's entered at my gate — has come to seek
h. o.
    me *here?*
d. o.
I 've *met* him, *faced* him, *scorned* him, when the fight
h. f.   rep.   d. l. p.
    was raging *hot;*—
d. o.

I 'll *try* his might, I 'll *brave* his power ! — *defy*, and
<small>h. f.   rep.   b. h. h. f.</small>
fear him *not !*
<small>b. h. d. f.</small>

" *Ho !* sound the *tocsin* from my tower, and fire the
<small>r. h. upl.   x. o. ind.</small>
   culverin ;
<small>a . l. ind.</small>
Bid each retainer arm with *speed ;* call every *vassal* in.
<small>   +   b. h. h. o.   b. h. d. o.</small>
Up with my banner on the wall, — the *banquet-board*
<small>r. h. upl.   h. o.</small>
   prepare,
Throw *wide* the portal of my hall, and bring my *armor*
<small>   h. l.   h. o. ind.</small>
   there ! ' "

An *hundred* hands were busy then : the banquet *forth*
<small>   b. h. h. o.   h. l.</small>
   was spread,
And rung the heavy oaken floor with many a martial
   tread ;
<small>b. h. d. o.</small>
While from the rich, dark tracery, along the *vaulted wall,*
<small>   h. o.</small>

Lights gleamed on harness, plume and spear, o'er the
<small>h. o. ind.</small>
   proud old Gothic hall.
<small>   h. l. ind.</small>

Fast *hurrying* through the outer gate, the mailed
<small>   h. o.</small>
   retainers poured,
<small>rep.</small>
On through the portal's frowning arch, and *thronged*
   around the board ;
<small>   b. h. h. o.</small>
While at its *head,* within his dark, carved, oaken chair
   of *state,*   <small>h. l.</small>
<small>imp.</small>
Armed cap-à-pie, stern *Rudiger,* with girded *falchion,* sat.
<small>   h. l. ind.   rep.</small>

" Fill every *beaker* up, my men !—*pour forth* the cheer-
            h. f.   h. o.
  ing wine !

There's life and strength in every *drop*,—*thanksgiving*
                        d. o.   b. h. h. o.
  to the vine !

Are ye all *there*, my vassals true ?—mine eyes are
         h. o.   drop.
  waxing dim :

Fill round, my tried and fearless ones, each goblet to
  h. o.
  the *brim !*
     rep.

" Ye're *there*, but yet I see you *not !*—forth draw each
    h. o.   d. o.
  trusty *sword*,
   h. o. ind.

And let me hear your faithful steel clash once around
  my *board !*
    b. h. h. o.

I hear it *faintly !*—*louder* yet ! What *clogs* my heavy
      r. h. ulp.   h. o.   d. o.
  breath ?

Up, all !—and shout for *Rudiger*, 'Defiance unto
 b. h. upl.   b. h. a. o.
  death !'"
  b. h. d. o. cli.

Bowl rang to *bowl*, steel clanged to *steel*, and rose a
        h. o. ind.   h. l. ind.
  deafening cry,

That made the *torches* flare around, and shook the *flags*
             a. l.   b.h.a.o.
  on high :

" *Ho !* cravens ! do ye *fear* him ? Slaves ! *traitors !*
b. h. upl.   b. h. h. o.   rep.
  have ye *flown ?*
     rep.

Ho ! cowards, have ye left me to meet him here *alone ?*
b. h. upl.   b. h. d. o.

"But I *defy* him!—let him *come!*" *Down* rang the
<small>h. f. cli.   rep.   d. o.</small>
massy cup,
While from its sheath the ready blade came *flashing*
<small>h. o. ind.</small>
half-way up;
And, with the black and heavy plumes scarce *trembling*
<small>h. o. p.</small>
on his head,
There, in his dark, carved, oaken *chair*, old Rudiger
<small>h. o. ind.</small>
sat—dead!
<small>drop.</small>

THE WOLVES.

J. T. TROWBRIDGE.

Ye that listen to *stories* told,
<small>h. o.</small>
When hearths are cheery and nights are cold,

Of the lone woodside, and the hungry *pack*,
<small>h. l.</small>
That howls on the fainting *traveler's* track,
<small>imp.</small>

The flame-red *eye-balls* that waylay
<small>h. l. ind.</small>
By the wintry moon, the belated sleigh;

The lost *child* sought in the dismal *wood*,
<small>h. o. b. p.   rep.</small>
The little *shoes*, and the stains of *blood*
<small>d. l.   d. l. p.</small>

On the trampled snow,—ye that hear

With thrills of *pity*, or chills of *fear*,
<small>h. o.   h. l.</small>

<small>II</small>

Wishing some kind *angel* had been sent

a. o.

To *shield* the hapless innocent,—

h. o. p.

Know ye the fiend that is *crueler* far

d. o.

Than the gaunt gray herds of the forest are?

Swiftly *vanish* the wild fleet tracks

h. l.

Before the rifle and the woodman's axe.

But *hark* to the coming of *unseen* feet,

r. h. upl.   h. o. p.

Pattering by night through the city street.

Each wolf that dies in the *woodland* brown,

h. l.

Lives a *spectre*, and haunts the *town!*

h. o. v.   h. o. ind.

By square and market they slink and *prowl*,

h. o.

In lane and alley they leap and *howl;*

h. l.

All night long they snuff and snarl before

The patched *window* and the broken *door.*

d. o.   d. l.

They paw the *clapboards*, and claw the *latch;*

h. f. p.   h. o. p.

At every *crevice* they whine and scratch.

h. l.

Children, crouched in *corners cold*,

h. o. p.

Shiver with tattered garments old;

rep.

They *start* from sleep with bitter pangs
r. h. upl.
At the *touch* of the phantom's viewless fangs.
h. o. p.

Weary the mother, and worn with *strife,*
d. l. d. o.
Still she watches and fights for *life ;*
d. f.

But her hand is *feeble* and her weapon *small,*—
h. o. rep.
One little *needle* against them *all.*
h. f. h. l.

In evil hour the *daughter fled*
h. l.
From her poor shelter, and wretched bed,

Through the city's pitiless solitude

To the door of *sin,*—the wolves pursued!
h. o. ind.

Fierce the father, and grim with *want,*
h. f. h. o. p.
His heart was gnawed by the *spectres* gaunt,
h. l. p.

Frenzied, stealing forth by night,
d. o. cli.
With whetted *knife* for the desperate fight,
a. o. cli.

He thought to strike the *spectres* dead,—
d. o. cli.
But killed his brother *man* instead.
d. o.

O ye that listen to *stories* told,
h. o.
When hearths are cheery and nights are cold,

Weep no more at the *tales* you hear,
         h. l.
The danger is *close*, and the wolves are *near!*
         h. f.   rep.

Shudder not at the *murderer's* name,
              h. f. p.
Marvel not at the *maiden's* shame;
            h. o. p.

Pass not by with *averted* eye,
              h. l. p.
The door where the stricken children cry.

But when the beat of the unseen feet

Sounds by night through the city street,

Follow thou, where the spectres glide,
 h. f.
And stand, like Hope, at the mother's *side;*
                                        h. o.

And be *thyself* the angel sent
       h. f.
To *shield* the hapless innocent.
    h. o. p.

He gives but *little* who gives his tears;
             d. l.
He gives best who aids and *cheers.*
                            d. o.

He does *well* in the forest wild
        h. l.
Who *slays* the monster and *saves* the child;
    d. l. p.   h. o.

He does *better*, and merits *more*,
        d. o.   rep.
Who *drives the wolf* from the poor man's door.
    h. l. v.

ANTONY'S ADDRESS TO THE ROMANS.

SHAKSPEARE.

Friends, Romans, countrymen, lend me your *ears;*
h. o.

I come to *bury* Cæsar, not to *praise* him.
d. o. h. l.

The *evil* that men do lives *after* them;
h. o. d. o.

The *good* is oft interred with their *bones;*
h. o. d. o. p.

So let it be with *Cæsar.* The noble *Brutus*
d. o. h. o.

Hath told you Cæsar was *ambitious:*
rep.

If it were so, it was a *grievous* fault,
h. l.

And grievously hath Cæsar *answered* it.
d. o.

Here, under *leave* of Brutus and the rest
h. f. h. o.

(For Brutus is an *honorable* man;
d. l.

So are they *all,* ALL honorable men),
b.h.d.o. b.h.d.l.

Come I to speak in Cæsar's *funeral.*
h. f.

He was my *friend,* faithful and *just* to me;
h. o. d. o.

But *Brutus* says he was *ambitious;*
h. l. rep.

And Brutus is an *honorable* man.
d. l.

He hath brought many *captives* home to Rome,
h. o.

Whose ransoms did the general *coffers* fill:
d. o.

Did *this* in Cæsar seem ambitious?
h. f.

When that the *poor* have cried, Cæsar hath *wept:*
h. o. h. o. p.

Ambition should be made of *sterner* stuff;
d. o.

Yet Brutus says he was *ambitious;*
h. o.

And Brutus is an *honorable* man.
d. o.

You did all see that on the Lupercal

I thrice presented him a kingly *crown,*
h. o.

Which he did thrice *refuse.*   Was *this* ambition?
d. l.   h. f.

Yet *Brutus* says he was ambitious;
h. o.

And sure *he* is an honorable man.
d. o.

I speak not to *disprove* what Brutus spoke,
d. l.

But here I am to speak what I do *know.*
d. f.

You all did *love* him once; not without *cause;*
h. o.   h. l.

What cause *withholds* you, then, to mourn for him?
d. o.

O *judgment!* thou art fled to brutish *beasts,*
h. f.   d. l.

And men have lost their *reason! , Bear* with me;
rep.   h. o.

My *heart* is in the coffin there with Cæsar,
d. o. p.

And I must pause till it come *back* to me.
d. o.

But *yesterday,* the word of Cæsar might
h. o.

Have stood against the *world :* now lies he *there,*
h. l.   d. o. ind.

And *none* so poor to do him reverence.
d. l.

O *masters !* if I were disposed to stir
b. h. h. o.

Your hearts and minds to mutiny and *rage,*
rep.

I should do *Brutus* wrong, and *Cassius* wrong,
h f. h. o.

Who, you all know, are *honorable* men.
d. o.

I will not do *them* wrong; I rather choose
h. l.

To wrong the *dead*, to wrong *myself*, and *you*,
d. o. h. on heart. h. o.

Than I will wrong such *honorable* men.
h. l.

But here 's a *parchment* with the seal of Cæsar;
h. f.

I found it in his *closet;* 't is his *will:*
h. o. d. o.

Let but the commons *hear* this testament
h. o.

(Which, pardon me, I do not mean to *read*),
h. l.

And they would go and *kiss* dead Cæsar's wounds,
d. l.

And dip their napkins in his sacred *blood;*
rep.

Yea, beg a *hair* of him for memory,
h. o.

And, dying, mention it within their *wills*,
h. l.

Bequeathing it as a rich legacy

Unto their *issue.*
d. o.

If you have *tears*, prepare to shed them *now.*
h. o. d. o.

You all do know this *mantle:* I remember
h. f.

The first time ever Cæsar put it *on;*
h. o.

'T was on a summer's evening, in his *tent* —
h. l.

That day he overcame the *Nervii.*
d. o.

Look! in this place ran Cassius' *dagger* through;
h. f ind. rep.

See what a rent the envious *Casca* made ;

rep.

Through *this*, the well-beloved Brutus stabbed ;

rep.

And, as he plucked his cursed steel away,

Mark how the *blood* of Cæsar followed it,

h. o. ind.

As rushing out of *doors*, to be resolved

h. l.

If Brutus so *unkindly* knocked or no ;

d. l.

For Brutus, as you know, was Cæsar's *angel :*

h. o.

Judge, O you gods, how dearly Cæsar *loved* him !

a. o.   rep.

This was the most *unkindest* cut of all ;

d. o.

For, when the noble Cæsar saw him stab,

Ingratitude, more *strong* than traitor's arms,

h. l.   d. o.

Quite *vanquished* him. Then burst his mighty *heart ;*

d. l.   b. h. h. o.

And, in his mantle muffling up his *face*,

h. o. p.

Even at the base of Pompey's *statue*,

d. o.

Which all the while ran *blood*, great Cæsar *fell*.

d. l.   d. o.

Oh, what a fall was there, my countrymen !

r. h. upl.

Then *I*, and *you*, and *all of us* fell down,

h. on heart.   h. o.   b. h. d. o.

While bloody *treason* flourished over us.

a. l. ind.

Oh, now you *weep ;* and, I perceive, you feel

h. o. p.

The dint of *pity :* these are *gracious* drops.

h. l. p.   d. l.

Kind souls, what, weep you, when you but behold

h. o.

Our Cæsar's *vesture* wounded ?   Look you *here ;*

d. o.   d. f. ind.
Here is *himself*, marred, as you see, with *traitors.*

rep   h. l.
   Good *friends*, sweet friends, let me not stir you up

   h. o.
To such a sudden flood of *mutiny.*

d. o.
They that have done this deed are *honorable :*

d. l.
What *private* griefs they have, alas ! I know *not,*

h. o.   d. o.
That made them do it ; they are wise and *honorable,*

h. l.
And will, no doubt, with *reasons* answer you.

d. o.
I come not, friends, to steal away your *hearts ;*

h. o.
I am no *orator*, as *Brutus* is ;

   h. l.   imp.
But, as you know me all, a plain, *blunt* man,

h. f.
That *love* my friend, and that they know full *well,*

h. o.   d. o.
That gave me public leave to *speak* of him ;

rep.
For I have neither wit, nor words, nor *worth,*

d. f.
Action, nor *utterance*, nor the power of *speech,*

d. o.   d. l.
To stir men's blood : I only speak *right on ;*

h. f.
I tell you that which you yourselves do *know ;*

h. o.
Show you sweet Cæsar's *wounds*, poor, poor dumb

   mouths,   d. f.
And bid them speak *for* me ; but, were I *Brutus,*

d. o.   h. o.
And Brutus *Antony*, there were an Antony

h. on heart.
Would *ruffle up* your spirits, and put a *tongue*

h. o. p.   d. o. ind.
  ·11*

In every *wound* of Cæsar, that should move
rep.
The *stones* of Rome to rise and *mutiny.*
d. o. cli.   rep.

THE CHARGE OF THE LIGHT BRIGADE.

TENNYSON.

Half a league, half a league,
r. h. upl.
Half a league *onward*,
h. f.
All in the valley of *Death*
b. h. d. o.
  Rode the six hundred.

" *Forward*, the Light Brigade !
h. f.
Charge for the *guns !*" he said :
h. f. ind.
Into the valley of *Death*
b. h. d. o.
  Rode the six hundred.

" *Forward*, the Light Brigade !"
h. f.
Was there a man *dismayed?*
h. o.
Not though the soldier knew

  Some one had *blundered:*
d. o.
Theirs not to make *reply*,
h. l.
Theirs not to reason *why*,
d. l.
Theirs but to do and *die*,
d. o.

Into the valley of *Death*
b. h. d. o.
   Rode the six hundred.

Cannon to *right* of them,
b. h. h. l. par. (right.)
Cannon to *left* of them,
b. h. h. l. par. (left.)
Cannon in *front* of them,
b. h. h. f.
   Volleyed and *thundered :*
b. h. a. o. p.
Stormed at with shot and shell,
b. h. a. f. p.
Boldly they rode and *well,*
b. h. h. f.   b. h. d. f.
Into the jaws of *Death,*
b. h. d. o.
Into the mouth of *Hell,*
b. h. d. f.
   Rode the six hundred.

Flashed all their sabres bare,
a. o.
Flashed as they turned in *air,*
a. l.
Sabring the *gunners* there,
h. o. ind.
Charging an *army,* while
b. h. h. o.
   All the world *wondered :*
b. h. h. l.
Plunged in the *battery*-smoke,
b. h. h. f.
Right *through* the line they broke ;
b. h. h. o.
Cossack and Russian

Reeled from the sabre-stroke
b. h. h. o. p.
   Shattered and *sundered.*
b. h. d. l. p.

Then they rode *back*, but not,

h. l.

Not the six hundred.

d. o.

Cannon to *right* of them,

b. h. h. l. par.

Cannon to *left* of them,

b. h. h. l. par. (left.)

Cannon *behind* them

b. h. h. o. b. par.

Volleyed and *thundered ;*

b. h. a. o. p.

Stormed at with shot and shell,

b. h. a. f. p.

While horse and hero *fell*,

b. h. d. o.

They that had fought so well,

Came through the jaws of *Death*,

rep.

Back from the mouth of *Hell*,

b. h. d. f.

All that was *left* of them —

d. l.

Left of six hundred.

drop.

When can their glory *fade ?*

h. o.

Oh the wild charge they made !

r. h. upl.

All the *world* wondered.

h. l.

Honor the charge they made !

a. o.

Honor the *Light Brigade*,

h. o.

Noble Six Hundred !

d. o.

CATILINE'S DEFIANCE.

CROLY.

Conscript *Fathers!*

h. o.

I do not rise to waste the night in *words;*

h. l.

Let that *plebeian* talk; 't is not *my* trade;

h. o. ind.   d. o.

But here I stand for *right,*— let him show *proofs,*—

d. f.   h. o.

For *Roman* right; though none, it seems, dare stand

d. f.

To take their *share* with me.   Ay, *cluster* there!

d. o.   b. h. h. f.

Cling to your *master,* judges, Romans, *slaves!*

rep.   b. h. d. f.

His charge is *false;*— I dare him to his *proofs.*

d. o.   h. o.

You have my *answer.*   Let my *actions* speak!

h. f.   h. o.

But *this* I will avow, that I *have* scorned,

h. f.   d. f.

And *still* do scorn, to hide my sense of wrong!

rep.

Who brands me on the *forehead,* breaks my *sword,*

h. f. ind.   rep.

Or lays the bloody scourge upon my *back,*

rep.

Wrongs me not *half* so much as he who shuts

d. o.

The gates of *honor* on me,— turning out

h. o. p.

The Roman from his *birthright;* and, for *what?*

h. l. p.   h. o.

To fling your offices to every *slave!*

h. l.

Vipers, that creep where man *disdains* to climb,

d. l. ind.   d. l. p.

And, having wound their loathsome track to the top

Of this huge, moldering monument of *Rome*,
fore arm v. ind., pointing v.

Hang *hissing* at the nobler man below!
arm in same position, ind. pointing downward.

Come, consecrated lictors, from your *thrones;*
b. h. h. f.   rep.

Fling down your *scepters;* take the rod and *axe*,
d. l.   h. o. cli.

And make the *murder* as you make the *law;*
d. o. cli.   h. o.

Banished from *Rome!*   What 's banished, but set free
d. o.

From daily contact of the things I *loathe?*
d. l.

" Tried and convicted *traitor!*"   *Who* says this?
d. o.   h. o.

Who 'll *prove* it, at his peril on my head?
d. o.

" *Banished!*"   I *thank* you for 't.   It breaks my *chain!*
h. o.   d. o.   d. l.

I held some slack *allegiance* till this hour;
d. o.

But *now* my sword 's my *own*.   *Smile on*, my lords;
h. f.   d. f.   h. o.

I *scorn* to count what *feelings*, withered *hopes*,
h. o. ind.   h. on heart.   rep.

Strong *provocations*, bitter, burning *wrongs*,
rep.   rep.

I have within my *heart's* hot cells shut up,
rep.

To leave you in your lazy *dignities*.
h. o. p.

But here I stand and *scoff* you! here I fling
h. o. ind.

Hatred and full *defiance* in your face!
h. o. cli.

Your consul 's *merciful*.   For this, all *thanks*,
d. o.   d. l.

He *dares* not touch a *hair* of Catiline!
h. o. ind.   rep.

" *Traitor!* " I *go* ; but, I *return*.   This — *trial!*
d. o.   d. l.   d. f.   h. f.

Here I devote your *senate!*   I 've had wrongs
h. o. ind.

To stir a fever in the blood of *age,*
d. o.

Or make the *infant's* sinews strong as *steel.*
h. o.   d. o. cli.

This day 's the birth of *sorrow!*   This hour's work
h. f.

Will breed *proscriptions!*   Look to your *hearths,* my
lords,   d. f.   h. l.

For *there,* henceforth, shall sit, for household gods,
h. l. ind.

Shapes hot from *Tartarus!* — all shames and *crimes!*
rep.   rep.

Wan *Treachery,* with his thirsty *dagger* drawn ;
rep.   rep.

Suspicion, poisoning his brother's cup ;
rep.

Naked *Rebellion,* with the torch and axe,
rep.

Making his wild sport of your blazing *thrones ;*
a. l.

Till Anarchy comes down on you like *night,*
b. h. h. o. p.

And Massacre seals Rome's eternal *grave.*
b. h. d. o. p.

I *go ;* but not to leap the gulf *alone.*
h. l.   d. o.

I *go ;* but, when I come, 't will be the burst
h. o.

Of *ocean* in the earthquake, — *rolling back*
b. h. h. o.   b. h. h. l. v. par.

In swift and mountainous ruin.   Fare you *well!*
h. o.

You build my *funeral-pile ;* but your best blood
h. l.

Shall *quench* its flame !   *Back,* slaves !   I will *return !*
h. o. cli.   h. o. v.   d. o. cli.

THE ANGELS OF BUENA VISTA.

WHITTIER.

Speak and *tell* us, our Ximena, looking *northward* far
away,   h. f.   h. o. ind.*

O'er the camp of the invaders, o'er the Mexican array,

Who is *losing?* who is *winning?* are they *far*, or come
    h. f.   h. o.   h. l.

they *near?*
    h. f.

Look *abroad*, and tell us, sister, *whither* rolls the storm
    h. o.   h. f.

we hear.

" Down the hills of *Angostura*, still the storm of battle
rolls,   h. o. ind.

Blood is flowing, men are *dying*, God have mercy on
    d. o.   d. l.

their *souls !*"
    a. f.

Who is *losing?* who is *winning?*   " Over hill and over
    h. f.   h. o.

plain,
    h. l.

I see but smoke of *cannon* clouding through the mountain rain."   h. o. p.

Holy *Mother*, keep our brothers!   *Look*, Ximena, look
    a. o.   h. o. ind.

once *more :*
    rep.

" Still I see the fearful whirlwind rolling *darkly* as before,
                         h. o. p.

---

* While the lateral, as distinguished from the front and the oblique, is the gesture
of *distance*, it is obvious that distance may be indicated in any direction.

Bearing on, in strange *confusion*, friend and foeman, foot and horse,
b. h. h. l. p. par.

Like some wild and troubled torrent sweeping down its *mountain course*."
b. h. d. l. p. par.

Look forth once *more*, Ximena! "Ah! the smoke has rolled *away*;
h. o.
h. l. p.

And I see the Northern *rifles* gleaming down the ranks of gray.
h o. ind.

Hark! that sudden blast of *bugles!* there the troop of
r. h. upl. ind.
h. o. ind.

Minon wheels;
rep.

There the Northern *horses* thunder, with the *cannon* at their heels.
rep.
rep.

"Jesu, *pity!* how it *thickens!* now *retreat* and now
r. h. upl.
h. o. p.
h. l. p.

advance!
h. o.

Right against the blazing *cannon* shivers Puebla's charging lance!
h. o. v.

Down they go, the brave young riders; horse and foot
d. o.

together fall;
rep.

Like a ploughshare in the fallow, through them *ploughs* the Northern ball."
h. o.

Nearer came the storm, and *nearer*, rolling fast and
h. o.
rep.

frightful on.
b. h. h. o. p.

Speak, Ximena, speak, and *tell us* who has *lost* and who
h. f
rep.
rep.

has *won:*
d. f.

"*Alas!* alas! I know not; friend and foe *together* fall;
b. h. upl.   b. h. d. o.
O'er the dying rush the *living; pray*, my sisters, for
                              b. h. h. o.   rep.
them *all!*
    rep.

"*Lo!* the wind the smoke is lifting; Blessed *Mother*,
r. h. upl.   a. o.
save my *brain!*
        h. on forehead.
I can see the *wounded* crawling slowly out from heaps
of *slain;*   h. o. p.
    imp.
Now they *stagger*, blind and *bleeding;* now they *fall,*
            rep.   rep.   d. o. p.
and strive to *rise;*
        h. o.
Hasten, sisters, haste and *save* them, least they die before
  h. f.   rep.
our *eyes!*
    rep.

"Oh, my *heart's* love! oh, my *dear* one! lay thy poor
        h. f.   rep.
head on my *knee;*
        rep.
Dost thou *know* the lips that kiss thee? Canst thou
            rep.
hear me? Canst thou *see?*
rep.   rep.
Oh, my *husband*, brave and gentle! oh, my *Bernard*,
        h. f.   rep.
look once more
On the blessed *cross* before thee! *Mercy!* mercy! all
                    rep.   r. h. upl.
is o'er."
    drop.

Dry thy *tears*, my poor Ximena; lay thy dear one down
            h. f.
to *rest;*
d. f.

Let his hands be meekly *folded*, lay the *cross* upon his
    breast; d. o. p.   rep.

Let his dirge be sung *hereafter*, and his funeral masses
    said; h. o.*

To-day, thou poor bereaved one, the *living* ask thy aid.
h. f.   rep.

Close beside her, faintly moaning, fair and young, a
    soldier lay,
d. o.

Torn with *shot* and pierced with *lances*, bleeding slow
d. o. p.   rep.
    his life away;

But, as tenderly before him the lorn *Ximena* knelt,
d. o.

She saw the Northern *eagle* shining on his pistol belt.
d. o. ind.

With a stifled cry of *horror*, straight she turned away
    her head; h. o. v.

With a sad and *bitter* feeling looked she back upon her
    dead; h. o. p.
rep.

But she heard the youth's low *moaning*, and his strug-
    gling breath of *pain*, d. o.
    d. o. p.

And she raised the cooling *water* to his parched lips
    again. h. o.

Whispering *low* the dying soldier, pressed her *hand*,
    h. o.   h. o. cli.
    and faintly smiled;

Was that pitying face his *mother's?* did *she* watch
    beside her child? h. o.   rep.

---

* Reference to the future here takes the oblique line; the sentence being treated
as a general assertion. By this notation, also, more emphasis is given to the succeeding sentence.

All his stranger words with meaning her woman's heart
  supplied;
   d. o.

With her *kiss* upon his forehead, "Mother!" murmured
    h o.

  he, and died.

"A bitter *curse* upon them, poor boy, who led thee forth
  h. l. ind.

From some gentle, sad-eyed *mother*, weeping *lonely* in
     the North!"   h. l.   h. l. p.

Spake the mournful Mexic woman, as she laid him with
  her *dead*,
   d. o.

And turned to soothe the *living* still, and bind the
  wounds which bled.   h. l.
  h. l. p.

Look forth once *more*, Ximena: "Like a cloud before
  the wind,   h. o.

Rolls the battle down the mountains, leaving blood and
     b. h. d. l. p. par.

  death behind;
  b. h. d. o.

Ah! they plead in vain for mercy; in the *dust* the
    b. h. upl.   b. h. d. o. p.

  wounded strive;

Hide your *faces*, holy angels! O, thou Christ of God,
    b. h. a. o. p.

  forgive."
  b. h. a. f.

Sink, O Night, among thy *mountains!* let the cool, gray
  shadows *fall;*   b. h. h. o. p.
  b. h. d. o. p.

Dying *brothers*, fighting demons, — drop thy curtain
  b. h. upl.

  over *all!*
  b. h. d. l. p.

Through the thickening winter twilight, wide apart the
battle *rolled,*
b. h. h. o.
In its *sheath* the sabre rested, and the cannon's lips grew
cold.   d. o.
d. o. p.

But the noble Mexic women still their holy task *pur-*
sued,   d. o.
Through that long, dark night of sorrow, worn, and
faint, and lacking *food;*
d. l.
Over weak and suffering brothers with a *tender care*
they hung,   h. o. p.
And the dying foeman blessed them in a strange and
Northern tongue.
h. l.

Not *wholly* lost, O Father! is this evil world of ours;
a. f.
Upward, through its blood and ashes, spring afresh the
Eden flowers;
a. o.
From its smoking hell of *battle* Love and *Pity* send their
prayer,   b. h. d. o.   b. h. h. o.
And still thy white-winged *angels* hover dimly in our
air.   b. h. a. o. p.

THE PERFECT ORATOR.

BRINSLEY SHERIDAN.

Imagine to yourselves a *Demosthenes,* addressing the
h. o.
most illustrious assembly in the *world* upon a point
h. l.
whereon the fate of the most illustrious of *nations*
d. o.

depended. *How awful* such a meeting! how *vast* the
r. h. upl.   h. l.

subject! Is man possessed of talents *adequate* to the
                 h. o.

great occasion? Adequate! Yes, *superior.* By the
              d. o.

power of eloquence the *augustness* of the assembly is
            h. l.

lost in the dignity of the orator, and the importance of
d. l.

the *subject* for a while superseded by the admiration of
   h. o.

his *talents.*
 d. o.

  With what strength of *argument,* with what powers
            h. f.

of the *fancy,* with what emotions of the *heart,* does he
  h. o.   h. l.

assault and *subjugate* the whole man, and at once cap-
     h. o. p.

tivate his reason, his imagination and his *passions!* To
              h. l.

effect this must be the *utmost* effort of the most *improved*
        d. f.   rep.

state of human nature. Not a faculty that he possesses

is here *unemployed;* not a faculty that he possesses but
   d. o.

is here exerted to its *highest pitch.* All his *internal*
        h. f.   b. h. h. f.

powers are at *work;* all his *external, testify* their energies.
     imp.   b. h. h. o. imp.

  Within, the memory, the fancy, the judgment, the
  h. f.

passions are all *busy.* *Without,* every *muscle,* every
      rep.   h. o.   rep.

nerve, is exerted; not a feature, not a limb, but *speaks.*
rep.   d. o.

The organs of the *body,* attuned to the exertions of the
       h. f.

mind through the kindred organs of the *hearers,* instan-
h. o.   h. l.

taneously vibrate those energies from soul to *soul.*
            b. h. h. o.

Notwithstanding the *diversity* of minds in such a
b. h. h. o.
multitude, by the lightning of eloquence they are melted

into *one mass;* the whole *assembly,* actuated in *one* and
b. h. h. f. p. b. h. h. l. b. h. h. f.
the *same* way, become, as it were, but one *man,* and
rep. rep.
have but one *voice.* The universal cry is: Let us
rep.
march against *Philip* — let us fight for our *liberties* —
b. h. h. o. b. h. a. o.
let us *conquer* or *die!*
rep. b. h. d. o.

ILLUSTRATED EXTRACT.

FIG. 92.

No fearing, *no doubting*, thy soldier
shall know,   h. l.

FIG. 93.

When *here* stands his country,
  h. f.

FIG. 94.

And *yonder her foe;*
h. l. ind.

FIG. 95.

One look at the bright *sun*,
  a. f.

FIG. 96.

One prayer to the *sky*,
b.h.a.o.

FIG. 97.

One glance where our *banner* waves
glorious on high ;   a. f. ind.

FIG. 98.

Then *on*, as the young lion bounds
b.h.h.f.
on his prey,

FIG. 99.

Let the sword flash on *high*,
a. o. ind.

FIG. 100.

Fling the scabbard *away;*
d. l.

FIG. 101.

Roll on, like the *thunderbolt* over
b. h. h. f.   rep.
the plain !

FIG 102.

We come back in *glory*,
b. h. a. l.

FIG. 103.

Or we come not *again.*
b. h. d. o.

RECENTLY PUBLISHED

BY

S. C. GRIGGS & CO.

GETTING ON IN THE WORLD: Or, HINTS ON SUCCESS IN LIFE. By WILLIAM MATHEWS, LL. D., Professor of Rhetoric and English Literature in the University of Chicago. Price $2.25.

The author has given to the public a book of surpassing interest.—*Inter-Ocean.*

The essays are unmistakably of marked excellence.—*Chicago Times.*

One of the very best books of the kind we know of.—*Chicago Advance.*

Each chapter is an essay, and is as practical in its teaching as it is elegant and impressive in its construction.—*Albany Evening Journal.*

THOMPSON'S FIRST LATIN BOOK. Introductory to Cæsar's Commentaries on the Gallic War. For use with Harkness', Andrews & Stoddard's, Bullion & Morris's, and Allen's Grammars. By DANIEL G. THOMPSON, A.M., late Teacher in the Springfield (Mass.) High School. 224 pages, 12mo. Price $1.50.

Sensibly and judiciously made.—*New York Nation.*

I like the plan of it much.—*Prof. W. S. Tyler, Amherst College.*

Mr. Thompson has hit upon what I have long regarded as the true method of teaching a foreign language. The plan is thoroughly excellent ; the execution of it is in all points admirable.—*Thomas Chase, Prof. of Philology, Haverford College.*

Think it will accomplish better results with the grammars which it is designed to accompany than any book we have.—*Geo. Henry Bliss, Green Mount Academy, Vt.*

The new plan pursued is a great improvement on the old method.　*　*　*
Its many other points of merit place it far beyond its present rivals.—*Prof. J. H. Blume, Jennings Seminary, Aurora, Ill.*

BOISE'S FIRST LESSONS IN GREEK. Adapted to Hadley's Greek Grammar, and intended as an introduction to Xenophon's Anabasis. By JAMES R. BOISE, Ph. D., Professor in the University of Chicago. Pages, 142. $1.25.

After nearly two terms' use, I feel prepared to say that it has no superior.—*Prof. C. G. Hudson, Genesee Wesleyan Seminary, Lima, N. Y.*

BOISE'S HOMER'S ILIAD. The First Six Books of Homer's Iliad: with Explanatory Notes intended for beginners in the Epic Dialect; accompanied with numerous references to Hadley's Greek Grammar, to Kuhner's larger Greek Grammar, and Goodwin's Moods and Tenses. By James R. Boise, Professor of Greek in the University of Chicago. $1.75.

A most valuable contribution to classical learning.—*Prof. W. W. Goodwin, Harvard University, Mass.*

For brevity, pertinence, and suggestiveness, I regard the notes as a model of classical annotation.—*Prof. H. B. Hackett, Rochester, N. Y.*

BOISE & FREEMAN'S SELECTIONS FROM VARIOUS GREEK AUTHORS. For the first year in College, with Explanatory Notes and References to Goodwin's Greek Grammar, and to Hadley's larger and smaller Grammars. By James R. Boise, Ph. D., and John C. Freeman, M.A., Professors in the University of Chicago. Pages, 393. Price $2.50.

Fulfils the expectation excited by his former works, and is admirably adapted to the purposes set forth in the preface. * * * Its use for a term has tended to increase my appreciation of its merits.—*Prof. N. L. Andrews, Madison University.*

JONES'S EXERCISES IN GREEK PROSE COMPOSITION. With References to Hadley's, Goodwin's and Taylor's-Kuhner's Greek Grammars, and a full English-Greek Vocabulary. By Elisha Jones, of the University of Michigan. Price $1.25.

I have no hesitation in saying that it will at once supply a great desideratum in the preparatory schools.—*Prof. A. H. Pattengill, University of Michigan.*

In no other way can my classes master the Greek syntax so well as by the use of these exercises.—*Prof. J. R. Boise, University of Chicago.*

It more than answers my expectation—being far superior to any book of the kind with which I am acquainted.—*Prof. John B. Dunbar, Washburn College, Topeka, Kan.*

A NORWEGIAN-DANISH GRAMMAR AND READER, With a Vocabulary, designed for American Students of the Norwegian-Danish Language. By Rev. C. I. P. Peterson, Norwegian Lutheran Pastor in Chicago, Professor of Scandinavian Literature, and Member of the Chicago Academy of Sciences. Price, $1.25.

When I affirm that I find myself able to translate the reading exercises with great readiness, it may be inferred how well the book is adapted to forward one in a knowledge of this interesting but neglected language.—*Prof. A. Winchell, Chancellor of Syracuse University.*

Lightning Source UK Ltd.
Milton Keynes UK
UKOW042044010212

186494UK00004B/32/P